Rainforests

by Lois Warburton

LUCENT
B·O·O·K·S

LUCENT *Overview Series*

OUR ENDANGERED PLANET

OUR ENDANGERED PLANET

Look for these and other books in the Lucent Overview series:

Acid Rain	Homeless Children
AIDS	Oil Spills
Animal Rights	The Olympic Games
The Beginning of Writing	Population
Dealing with Death	Rainforests
Drugs and Sports	Smoking
Drug Trafficking	Soviet-American Relations
Endangered Species	Special Effects in the Movies
Energy Alternatives	Teen Alcoholism
Garbage	The UFO Challenge
Hazardous Waste	Vietnam

The author would like to thank Michael H. Robinson, director of the Smithsonian Institution's National Zoological Park for his invaluable assistance

Library of Congress Cataloging-in-Publication Data

Warburton, Lois, 1938-
    Rainforests / by Lois Warburton.
        p. cm. — (Lucent overview series)
    Includes bibliographical references and index.
    ISBN 1-56006-150-2
    1. Rain forest ecology—Juvenile literature.   2. Forest conservation—Juvenile
literature   3. Rain forests—Juvenile literature.   I. Title. II. Series.
  QH541.5.R27W37   1991
  574.5'2642—dc20   90-46278

To my husband,
Harry Manning,
my reserve of love and support

Contents

Introduction

SINCE 1900 MORE than half of the earth's rainforests have been destroyed. Most of that destruction has occurred since 1950. Alarmed by data assembled from 1977 satellite photographs and released in 1980, the world's scientists have been trying to warn the public about the ever-increasing destruction. Some scientists reported losses that ranged from thirty-five acres a minute to twenty-eight million acres each year. At that rate, they concluded that no rainforests would be left in forty years.

The world's leaders heard those warnings and began making plans to save the rainforests. Those plans gave the scientists reason to hope the rainforests might survive. But their hopes were dealt a severe blow in June 1990 when new satellite data from 1987 photographs were released. The data revealed that tropical rainforests are vanishing up to 50 percent faster than previously thought. At present, between forty and fifty million acres of rainforest are being destroyed every year.

Reasons for destruction

There are many complex reasons for this destruction. At the heart of the matter is the fact that the rainforests are located mainly in poor,

(opposite page) Much of the rainforest is cut down by the natives of still-developing countries, who need the land to grow food.

7

The push to save the rainforest from destruction must be balanced with the needs of inhabitants of rainforest countries, many of whom are very poor.

still-developing countries. Inhabitants abuse the valuable resources of the forests to survive. The people of these countries must use the land in the rainforests to grow food. In addition, the governments that run the countries must export rainforests products, such as lumber, for money. But both farming and logging destroy vast areas of rainforest every year. In turn, that destruction causes other problems that affect every nation, not just the Third World countries that own the rainforests. Scientists believe destruction of the rainforests is contributing to the greenhouse effect that is causing the earth's temperature to rise. Higher temperatures are causing the extinction of valuable plants and animals and contributing to floods that kill many people every year. Finding ways to save the rainforests while keeping the interests of the developing countries that own them in mind is the most complicated problem of all. But the complexity of this situation is small compared to the complexity of the rainforest itself.

The rainforest is so complex that even the experts do not claim to understand it completely. Scientists are rushing to solve its mysteries before it is too late, and every day brings new discoveries. One of the most important discoveries is that the rainforest is a closed system. This means that the forest sustains itself. It provides its own nutrients and creates its own climate. If any part of this delicately balanced system is disturbed, the supply of nutrients and rain is disrupted and the survival of the rainforest is threatened. Furthermore, scientists estimate that 50 to 90 percent of all the world's plants and animals live in rainforests. Each of those millions of species is dependent upon other species for survival. This maze of interdependency means that removing just one species may threaten the survival of many other plants and animals living in the forest.

The rainforest is very fragile and intricate. It took millions of years to develop. Simply by cutting down its largest trees for lumber, for example, people can destroy the rainforest in our lifetime. Rainforests are one of the world's most valuable resources. They will not survive unless people in both the developed and developing countries understand them and their importance and take steps now to save them. An ancient Amazon legend says, "The rainforest supports the sky; cut down the trees, and disaster follows." This legend may become an accurate prediction.

1

Inside the Rainforest

A WALK IN a tropical rainforest is a journey into what may be one of the world's last unexplored frontiers. Even during the day, a rainforest is a dark place, for a lush, green maze of trees, vines, moss, and ferns prevents sunlight from reaching the ground. The lack of sun keeps the ground level, or floor, of the rainforest fairly clear of vegetation, so walking is not difficult. But the humid, breezeless air, filled with flying insects and the musty smell of rotting plants, quickly drenches human visitors with sweat. Inside this gigantic, mysterious greenhouse, it is strangely silent, until suddenly, now and then, a loud noise booms forth from an unseen source. At that moment, a visitor who glances quickly up into the palms, immature trees, and tall shrubs of the understory, which is the middle layer of the rainforest, might be rewarded with a brief glimpse of an agile monkey or a brightly colored bird. Many visitors, however, never see the multitude of animal life in the rainforest, except for the ever-present insects. The birds, monkeys, snakes, and sloths seen in zoos and jungle movies are usually hidden high in the treetops of the canopy, the top layer of vegetation. There, the thick fo-

(opposite page) If rainforest destruction continues at its current rate, scenes like this may become increasingly rare.

11

liage of the tallest trees forms a green roof over the rainforest. As a result, casual observers often find the rainforest disappointing. But trained observers have found more beauty, life, and mystery in the rainforest than can be found almost anywhere else on earth.

Scientific disagreement

Because in-depth study of tropical rainforests is relatively new, experts do not always agree about the facts. For example, some experts say that more than 50 percent of all animal and plant species in the world live in the rainforest; other experts say that figure is as high as 90 percent. No one will actually know for sure until the study of the rainforest has become a more exact science. In the meantime, almost all figures about the rainforest are estimates. Scientists even disagree about what a rainforest is.

In general, though, experts use average temperature and amount of rainfall to define rainforests. For a tropical rainforest to exist, the temperature must be high, averaging eighty degrees Fahrenheit, and constant, except for some cooling at night. The rainfall must be at least 160 inches a year, although sometimes it is as high as 400 inches, and must fall regularly throughout the year, with no dry season. It is always summer where these vast hothouses are located.

The world's tropical rainforests extend in a broken band around the equator and are concentrated mainly in Latin America, West Africa, and Southeast Asia. Smaller patches also grow in countries such as Australia, India, and the island of Madagascar off the east coast of Africa. A few thousand years ago, rainforests covered 14 percent of the earth; more than half of these have been destroyed. It is estimated that less than three million square miles remain.

The thick foliage of the tallest trees forms the canopy, a rooflike covering over the rainforest.

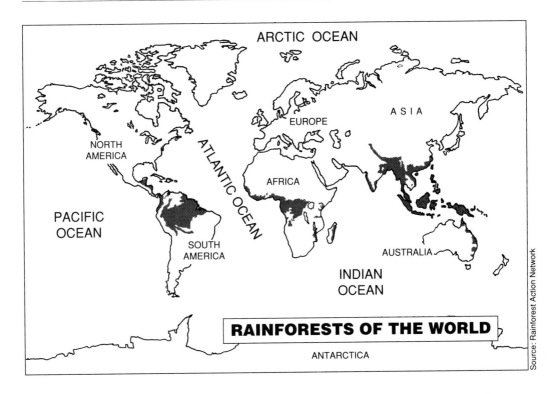

Source: Rainforest Action Network

RAINFORESTS OF THE WORLD

More than half of these rainforests are centered around the Amazon River in South America. Most of these are in Brazil, but they spread into Ecuador, Bolivia, Peru, Colombia, Venezuela, and Guyana in South America and up through the Central American countries of Panama, Costa Rica, Honduras, El Salvador, Nicaragua, Guatemala, and Belize and into Mexico. No one is really sure just how much rainforest remains in Latin America, but most estimates range between 1.3 and 1.9 million square miles.

The second largest rainforest area is in the Southeast Asian countries of Indonesia, Malaysia, Papua New Guinea, and the Philippines. These rainforests cover an estimated 500,000 square miles, about one-fifth of the world's total. The African rainforests, the third largest in area, are concentrated mainly in the Congo River basin and may cover approximately 400,000 square miles,

Most of the world's rainforests, shown here in the dark areas on the map, are located in Latin America, West Africa, and Southeast Asia.

Aerial view of a portion of the Amazon River in northern Brazil. More than half of the world's rainforests are centered around the Amazon River.

or one-sixth of the world's total. But estimates vary considerably, from as low as 380,000 square miles to as high as 690,000.

Types of rainforests

Rainforests grow on mountains, seacoasts, plains, and in river valleys, and experts have given different names to the tropical forests that grow in these areas. For example, cloud forests grow high in the mountains, cloaked in clouds and mist. Mangrove forests lie on the edge of the sea, where the mangrove trees are regularly flooded. Another type of rainforest, the jungle, can grow in any area. In fact, many people mistakenly call all rainforests jungles. But true tropical rainforests are primary forests, or forests that have remained undisturbed for thousands of years. They will remain primary forests as long as they are left undisturbed. Jungles are secondary rainforests, or forests that have lost their canopy trees. In almost every case, it is people who create jungles by cutting down the trees. Once the canopy is gone, the sun shines directly on the floor-dwelling plants, and they use this new source of energy to multiply and spread rapidly. Unlike primary rainforests, jungles are full of thick, tangled undergrowth, which makes walking through them extremely difficult.

When any of these rainforests are located near the equator, they are called equatorial rainforests. Farther from the equator, they blend into a type of tropical rainforest officially called tropical moist forests. The rainfall there is between 40 and 160 inches annually, their temperature is less constant, and they have a dry season when most of the trees lose their leaves. These forests also contain fewer species of plants and animals. Although this makes them somewhat less complex than the equatorial rainforests, most experts refer to both together as the tropical rainforest.

The tropical rainforest has an extraordinarily complex ecosystem. *Ecosystem* is the term for the interrelationships among all the parts of one particular environment. This includes the natural events in the environment that influence its climate. It also includes the way in which all the living things, or organisms, interact with one another and with the environment. The more living things there are in an environment, the more interaction there is and the more complex the ecosystem becomes. Because experts think the majority of the world's animal and plant species live in the tropical rainforest, its ecosystem is considered the most complex on earth. Every species in the ecosystem is dependent upon one or more other species for survival.

Mangrove trees send vine-like roots from their trunks and branches into surrounding mud. The roots are important because they catch the debris and sedimentary soil that are important for stabilizing a shoreline.

Palm trees, tall shrubs, and immature trees make up the understory, the middle layer of the rainforest.

Scientists have only recently begun to unravel these many mysterious networks of interdependency in the rainforest. The most important network is the chain of natural events that provides the rainforest with its nutrients and rain. Without these events, the rich diversity of life and even the rainforest itself could not exist. The mystery of that network begins on the ground, in the soil. For years, visitors to the rainforest assumed the soil was very rich. They thought it had to be to support all that tropical growth. But when scientists finally analyzed it, they found the soil to be among the poorest on earth. It is so ancient that all the minerals and other nutrients have been leached out, leaving it weathered and infertile. The mystery of how such poor soil can produce such huge, lush vegetation was solved by experts who discovered that the rainforest is a closed, or self-sustaining, system. It does not depend on outside sources for its nutrients or the frequent rain that gives it its name. The rainforest produces its own nutrients and its own climate.

A completely recyclable environment

The success of this closed system is mind-boggling. Studies have shown that the living plants and trees themselves contain somewhere between 75 and 90 percent of all the nutrients in the rainforest, and they recycle those nutrients with almost 100 percent efficiency. The minute a leaf, branch, or tree dies and falls to the ground, it is attacked by bacteria, other microorganisms, and fungi such as mushrooms and toadstools. Worms, grubs, beetles, snails, ants, and termites that live in the fallen logs and leaf litter join in the feast. Within a very short time, the dead plant has been decomposed and recycled into nutrients that can be reabsorbed by the trees and plants. As a result, the leaf litter is never more than a few inches thick.

To help take advantage of this fast decay, the trees and plants have a way to absorb the nutrients quickly. Instead of wasting energy sending roots deep into the soil where there are few nutrients, they spread many thin, hairlike roots along the ground. These roots grow rapidly into any decaying matter and absorb the nutrients as soon as they are available. These millions of intertwined root hairs form a root mat on top of the ground. This mat, along with the microorganisms that live in it, is, in effect, the rich, living soil of the tropical rainforest. In some places, that mat can be more than one foot thick, and the hair roots may even grow up tree trunks so they can absorb the rainwater that drips down the trunks almost every day. The minerals in that rainwater are another important source of nutrients.

The water itself is an integral part of the closed system because the rainforest, to a large extent, creates its own rain. Simply put, what happens is

Diagram shows how nutrients are recycled with remarkable efficiency in the closed system of the rainforest: 1) Leaves, branches, and dead trees fall to the ground. 2) The dead plants and trees are attacked by microorganisms, fungi, worms, beetles, and other insects. 3) The debris is decomposed and recycled into nutrients that can be reabsorbed by the trees and plants.

that approximately one-half to three-quarters of the rain that falls on the rainforest stays on the leaves of the tallest trees in the canopy. The burning sun quickly evaporates the water back into the atmosphere, and the evaporated moisture gathers in clouds and falls again as recycled rain.

Little of that rain falls directly on the floor of the rainforest. A person walking on the ground may feel only some fine mist even when a storm is raging overhead. In order to make good use of the rain that does stay in the rainforest, the trees and plants have a number of specialized characteristics. Many have thick leaves that provide storage space for water and nutrients. Those leaves are also often tough and glossy, which prevents the water from sitting on them and slowly leaching the nutrients back out. Many plants go a step further and have pointed, indented drip tips at the ends of their leaves to funnel the water off. This also helps keep the leaves free of attack from algae, lichens, and mosses that grow in

Many of the plants' leaves have pointed, indented "drip tips," which prevent the collection of moisture. This feature prevents mosses and algae from growing on the plants.

moisture. As the rainwater drips off the leaves and down the trees, some of it is absorbed directly into the trunks, for rainforest trees have thin bark that makes absorption easy. The water that reaches the ground is absorbed by the roots in the spongy root mat. Very little water and very few nutrients go to waste in this efficient system.

Interdependent plantlife

The network of interdependency among the rainforest's plants and animals is just as amazing and mysterious. Take, for example, the climbing vines called lianas. They depend upon trees to reach the sunlight they need for survival. Lianas include plants as diverse as passionflowers, rattans, philodendron, members of the cucumber family, and *Strychnos toxifera*, the source of the deadly poison strychnine. They come in a variety of shapes (round, flat, twisted, wavy), sizes (up to as thick as a human body), and lengths (up to three thousand feet long). One of the most common types of plants in the rainforest, lianas grow everywhere. They begin as seeds on the forest floor and grow upward until they meet a tree trunk. By attaching themselves to the tree with tendrils, hooks, or sucker roots or by winding around the tree, they continue to grow toward the sun. But they do not stop growing when they reach the top of the canopy. They continue growing upward into the air until they are pulled down by their own weight. Then they may grow down a second tree, along the ground, around other lianas, and up still another tree, binding the trees and vines together in a maze of twisted wood and leaves. In most cases, lianas do not harm their hosts. In fact, they provide additional support for the shallow-rooted trees they grow on. But when one of the intertwined trees dies, the linking vines may pull several other trees down with it when it falls.

Climbing vines, called lianas, must attach themselves to trees to survive.

The curious plants called epiphytes are even more dependent on other plants. They actually grow on their hosts, but they are not parasites. Epiphytes do not harm their hosts but use them for support and gather some of the water and nutrients they need from the host's surface.

Epiphytes grow at all three levels of the rainforest, adorning tree trunks, branches, and leaves and adding considerably to the denseness of the vegetation. Epiphytes live on the surface of other plants and do not send roots into the ground. The world's rainforests contain more than fifty thousand species of epiphytes, including mosses, ferns, bromeliads, and spectacular orchids. These plants have many special features to help them survive in their precarious position. For instance, orchids have two types of roots: one grips the host for support while the other, covered with a water-absorbing tissue, hangs down freely to gather water and nutrients from the air. Bromeliads have thick, waxy leaves that form a basin that catches water and debris. This mixture eventually forms a type of soil inside the basin that provides the plants with such a good source of nutrients that some bromeliads grow big enough to hold over twelve gallons of water.

Stranglers

Although epiphytes are not parasites, there is another common type of rainforest plant that is. Stranglers, most of which are members of the fig family, start life as epiphytes but eventually send long roots down to anchor in the ground. With this additional source of food and support, a strangler grows fast and ultimately surrounds its host from top to bottom, smothering and starving it. The host tree dies, leaving the huge strangler with a hollow core but healthy and upright.

This tangle of trees, shrubs, lianas, epiphytes, and stranglers is home to a great variety of animals. They are dependent on the vegetation for their food, protection, and sometimes reproduction. Insects are everywhere, flying through the air, crawling on leaves and branches, hiding in flowers, even breeding in the water collected in the epiphytes. Tree boas wrap themselves around tree limbs and wait motionless for their next victim. Tiny hummingbirds flit from flower to flower gathering nectar, while woodpeckers tap away at weak branches to make holes for nests. Monkeys swing from branch to branch, occasionally grabbing a particularly sweet-smelling fruit. Sloths slowly inch their way along branches toward clumps of green leaves. Thanks to the bromeliads' basins, even frogs and salamanders find a watery home in the trees.

Food and shelter are always available because the tropical rainforest has no seasons. Every day is the same. Rather than lose all its leaves at once, a rainforest tree loses them one at a time and is constantly growing new ones. Somewhere in the rainforest, every day of the year, at least one

Of the fifty thousand species of epiphytes, one is the orchid. While supported by a host, the orchid can hang freely in the air and gather nutrients.

The beetle is among many organisms that feed on fallen leaves and branches, recycling nutrients back into the rainforest.

species of tree is covered with huge, brightly colored blossoms, while another species is loaded with sweet-tasting fruit, and still others have already dropped their seeds and are resting until the next blooming cycle. Rainforest dwellers never need to wander far from their home territory to search for food, and that is why, for instance, tropical birds do not migrate.

Plants and animals are interdependent

The plants, in turn, are just as dependent on the animals, for without them they could not reproduce. That emerald green hummingbird hovering over the brilliant red flowers of a tree will get covered with pollen while it drinks the blossom's nectar. When it flies off to the next red-flowered tree, it carries the pollen with it, and some of the pollen falls onto that tree's flowers. The hummingbird has been fed, and the tree has been fertilized and can now form the seeds from which new trees will sprout.

If the seeds that form were all to drop and sprout directly under their parent tree, most of them would not survive. The competition for space, light, and nutrients would be too tough. The trees depend on animals to scatter their seeds. Monkeys grabbing juicy, ripe fruit may carry them safely away from the other greedy members of their troop before settling down to eat. The seed pits they discard fall to the ground at a distance from the parent tree. When ripe fruits do fall under their parent tree, the seeds are often eaten by the peccaries, a type of pig, small rodents, tiny deer, or other animals that inhabit the floors of various rainforests. The seeds go through their digestive systems intact and are scattered in their excrement throughout the rainforest.

These acts of interdependency are not accidental. They are all survival techniques developed by the millions of plant and animal species that live in the ecosystem of primary tropical rainforests. Much of the earth was covered with rainforests as long ago as forty-five million years, so those techniques have had millions of years to develop. As a result, they have had time to become very complex and specific. The trees have developed sweet fruit because that is what some animals prefer to eat. Because hummingbirds are attracted to red, some trees have developed blossoms that are not only red but are also shaped in a way that ensures hovering hummingbirds will get pollen on their feathers.

One of the most common survival techniques is camouflage. Much in the rainforest is not what it seems. Many species survive by looking like something else. Bugs disguised as green thorns

While eating a tree's fruit, monkeys often scatter the seeds far and wide, helping to repopulate the tree's species.

The Dobson Fly is able to fool its enemies by blending in with the corydalis plant.

on tree trunks are dependent on the presence of thorny plants for their success. Toads that look like fallen leaves are dependent on the presence of leaf litter. The Malaysian praying mantis lives in the canopy where there are blooms on the trees most of the time and looks just like a tube-shaped, pink flower. The mantis depends on the blooming of the trees to hide from hungry birds. Another technique, mimicry, allows a harmless species to survive by looking like another species that is poisonous or dangerous. Birds love to eat the many colorful butterflies fluttering through the rainforest, but some of those butterflies are poisonous. After eating a few of the poisonous ones, the birds learn to recognize them by their color patterns and avoid them. So some nonpoisonous butterflies fool the birds by looking like the poisonous species. If the poisonous butterflies were to disappear, this mimicry would be useless.

Sloths

As experts continue to uncover the mysteries of the rainforest, they are finding more and more survival techniques that involve interdependencies among rainforest species. Many are incredibly complex. One amazing example of interdependency involves a species of moth that depends on two species of sloths. Sloths live in the canopy, and the algae that grows in their fur turns it green, providing the sloths with camouflage in their leafy home. Because they eat leaves that are hard to digest, food stays in their systems for up to a month before all the value has been extracted from it. It is this slow metabolism, or release of energy from food, that causes the slow movements sloths are famous for. Partly because of their slowness, sloths make a very good home for a species of moth that lives in its fur. Up to 132 adult moths have been found living on one sloth.

Experts think the moths eat algae-rich rainwater trapped in the sloth's fur or some bodily secretions. They also think the moths breed there. But they could never find any moth eggs or larvae on the sloths. And then they found out why. Once every week or two, the sloths make a long, slow, dangerous journey down to the floor of the rainforest to defecate in a hole they dig with their tails. As soon as they do this, the moths swarm out of the fur to deposit their eggs on the sloth's dung and then settle back into the sloth's fur for the ride up into the canopy again. The larvae that hatch from the eggs feed on the dung, and when they turn into adult moths, they fly up into the canopy in search of a sloth to live on. Although it is clear that the moths are dependent on the sloths, what the sloths gain from this relationship is not immediately apparent. Perhaps the moths help keep the fur clean. Perhaps they add to the camouflage of the sloths. The answer is just one of the rainforest mysteries waiting to be solved.

All these interdependencies illustrate how rainforest animal and plant species specialize in order

A species of moth finds the features of the sloth, shown here, particularly well-suited to its needs. The moth lives in the fur of the sloth, leaving only long enough to lay its eggs.

to survive. With millions of species competing for food, space, and the opportunity to reproduce, each species has had to find its own environmental niche. A niche is a place in the environment where the species has as little competition and as much guarantee of food and protection as possible. The species of moth discussed above has found its niche on two species of sloths on which no other species live. The niche for the praying mantis that looks like a flower is in the canopy. On the ground where there are few flowers, the mantis would be very conspicuous and quickly devoured.

Specialization has created an extremely efficient ecosystem in the rainforest. Every corner, every niche, no matter how small or improbable,

Tropical birds, like this African Grey Parrot, can live in the constant climate of the rainforest year round.

supports life of some kind. This abundant life uses every possible source of food. But because there are millions of species and the space is limited, each species is relatively rare. There can be more than one hundred different species of trees in one square acre of tropical rainforest, but each of those species might be represented by only one tree. And that is not the only reason many rainforest plants and animals are rare. Many species live in one small area of the world and nowhere else. There are species of rainforest birds that live only in one mountain range and species of flowers that grow on only one island.

The rarer a species is, the more easily it can become extinct. When the highly specialized niche of a rare species is disturbed or destroyed, that species is doomed to extinction. For instance, a lumber company may think it is conserving the rainforest by cutting down just one species of tall timber tree and leaving the other trees standing. But that tree may be the one with the red blossoms that the hummingbird depends on for its nectar. It may be the only species of tree that provides the protection needed by the praying mantis. Its leaves may be the only food eaten by another species. Those species and all the species that depend on them will also be in danger.

Rainforest destruction is threatening the survival of millions of plant and animal species, but they are not the only things that will disappear if the rainforest is not saved. The cultures of people who have lived in the rainforest for thousands of years will also be destroyed.

2

People of the Rainforest

THE INDIGENOUS, OR native, people of the rainforest are part of the forest's mystery. Often these people are the original inhabitants of the areas where they live and are called aborigines. Anthropologists are scientists who are experts in the study of human cultures, and they estimate there are about one thousand different rainforest tribes in the world. They believe some small, undiscovered tribes still live deep in a few rainforests. As modern civilization pushes farther into the rainforest, however, those unknown tribes will gradually be discovered. In the 1970s, for instance, when Brazil built the Trans-Amazon Highway through its rainforest, new tribes were discovered at the rate of one per year.

Many of these rainforest tribes had never had contact with the outside world before they were discovered. The rainforest was their entire world. Anthropologists have rushed to study these tribes before their cultures are changed completely by contact with modern civilization. As a result, anthropologists have learned a great deal about how people can live in harmony with the rainforest ecosystem.

Rainforest people have adapted to their envi-

(opposite page) Destruction of the rainforest threatens many species of insects, plants, and animals, and also disrupts the cultures of the rainforest natives.

29

ronment extremely well. After thousands of years of living in the rainforest, they understand the ecosystem thoroughly and know their own section of the rainforest intimately. In fact, many recognize every individual tree in their home territory. If they were blindfolded and led in circles through the tangled vegetation, they would know exactly where they were when the blindfolds were taken off. This intimate knowledge enables the tribes to get their food, clothing, medicine, and other things necessary for survival from the plants and animals in the rainforest. These people are totally dependent on the rainforest. Without it, their culture could not exist.

Hunter-gatherers

Some of these tribes are hunter-gatherers who get their food by hunting animals and by gathering wild plants. The cultures of the hunter-gatherers are probably the oldest existing cultures in the world today. Their tribes are scattered around the globe and include the Negritos in Malaysia, the Mava in New Guinea, and the Tasaday in the Philippines. Perhaps the most successful rainforest hunter-gatherer tribes are the pygmies of Africa, whose tribes include the Efe, Aka, and Mbuti. There are between 150,000 and 200,000 pygmies still living in the countries of Cameroon, the Central African Republic, and Zaire.

Colin Turnbull and other anthropologists have studied the Mbuti extensively. Their home is the Ituri rainforest of Zaire. The Mbuti know the rainforest plants and their properties very well. If a member of the tribe becomes ill, they know which plants reduce high fevers, which contain natural antibiotics for cuts, and which cure stomach aches. They also know which plants work for birth control. The Mbuti use plants for entertainment as well. The children know how to make

This Amazon native is making a snare of bamboo daggers tipped with poisonous curare.

whistles out of fruits and toy tops out of nuts. There is plenty of time to play, plenty of time for the families to gather together to tell stories and sing songs about the rainforest, for the bountiful rainforest makes life easy.

The Mbuti call themselves "the children of the forest" and feel they are indebted to the rainforest for being so good to them. Since the rainforest is their "parent," they believe it watches over them at all times and protects them. When something bad happens, they think the rainforest has gone to sleep. To wake it up so it can take care of them again, they sing to it and call it "mother" or "friend." They consider themselves such a part of the rainforest that they believe when the rainforest dies, its children will also die.

Anthropologist Colin Turnbull has extensively studied the Mbuti, a hunter-gatherer tribe in Zaire, Africa.

The culture of the Mbuti is changing somewhat because of trade with neighboring tribes and contact with the outside world. One of the things they trade to these neighboring tribes is their intimate knowledge of the rainforest. Other tribes acknowledge the Mbuti's special relationship with the rainforest and ask them to serve as judges in tribal disputes, wise men at ceremonies, and guides. In return, they give the Mbuti cloth for clothing and metal for axes and arrowheads. Despite outside influences, the Mbuti remain rainforest dwellers. They have chosen to maintain their own culture.

Shifting cultivators

Some other rainforest tribes are farmers. These tribes, such as the Senoi of Malaysia, the Guaica and Waura of the Amazon, and the Lacandon Maya in southeastern Mexico, practice a form of farming called shifting cultivation. The Lacandon Maya, or Lacandones, are experts at this type of farming, which involves rotating crops from one field to another to take advantage of temporary nutrients in the rainforest's poor soil.

They must first clear a field of about 2.5 acres in the rainforest, which is a difficult, time-consuming task. The farmers start by chopping away the underbrush so they can get to the trees to cut them down. Once the trees are down, they abandon the field for about a month so that all the dead vegetation can dry. Then they light huge fires and burn all the vegetation. The ash from that fire, because it contains all the nutrients that were in the plants, provides temporary fertilizer for the field.

Their next step is to plant the first crops immediately so that torrential rains will not erode the field and wash away the ash. The Lacandones plant tree crops like bananas and root crops like sweet potatoes that help hold the soil in place. Then, once these crops are established, they fill the rest of the field with such crops as sugarcane, onions, pineapples, tobacco, rice, cacao, squash, and beans. They grow a variety of plants in each field because different plants use different nutrients. In combination, the various plants can get the most out of all the nutrients in the soil. But the Lacandones do not plant everything at once. They rely on the rainforest to tell them when it is time to plant each crop. The rainforest is their calendar. Experience gained from living in the rainforest for thousands of years has taught them how to read that calendar accurately. When one kind of tree in the rainforest comes into bloom, they know, it is time to plant one crop. When the blooms fall from another kind of tree, it is time to plant another crop. For instance, when the mahogany tree loses its blooms, the Lacandones know it is time to plant corn.

Rebuilding the rainforest

After the field has been used for three to five years, the soil will be exhausted, and the farmers will not be able to cultivate it anymore. They will have to clear a new field. But the old field does not go to waste. The Lacandones plant orange or rubber trees on it. Seeds from the rainforest plants sprout on the cleared land between those trees, and secondary rainforest begins to reclaim the land. In the ten years or so it takes the rainforest plants to grow big and thick enough to overrun the orange and rubber trees, the farmer benefits from the harvests. Then the field is ready to be burned again and recycled into farmland.

All shifting cultivators farm in a similar manner. And even though rainforest soil in some areas of the world is so poor that the cleared fields can be used for only two to three years, very little rainforest is destroyed by this process. Since the same fields can be used again every ten to twenty years, each farmer eventually has five to ten fields cleared and does not have to chop down any more primary rainforest. The number of natives is small

Aioura, chief of a Meinaco tribe in the Upper Xingu Basin of the Amazon River, leads a fishing expedition in one of the numerous rivers of the region. The Indians support themselves chiefly by growing manioc and by fishing.

At the start of each rainy season, tribesmen, such as these from the Upper Xingu Basin, play flutes to drive away evil spirits.

compared to the total amount of rainforest available, so tribes who practice shifting cultivation do not endanger the rainforest.

Like the hunter-gatherers, the shifting cultivators know the rainforest well. They, too, go into it to hunt animals and gather wild fruits, palm tree hearts, and vines. They use it as a source of clothing, shelter, and medication. It is their home, and they have learned to live in harmony with it. They respect the rainforest and conserve its resources. The homes of most of the rainforest tribes and their way of life are now threatened. In many of the world's rainforests, people from outside the forest who have moved in to obtain farmland now far outnumber the native tribes. The majority of those new settlers do not value the rainforest's ecosystem and do little to try to understand or preserve it. In addition, settlers place little value on the native tribes, often fearing them and considering them subhuman. They want the natives off the land. This has led to atrocities against the tribes, particularly in Latin America.

Mistreatment of natives

An investigation by the Brazilian government in 1968 discovered that several tribes had been almost wiped out by germ warfare between 1957 and 1963 when smallpox, influenza, and tuberculosis were deliberately introduced into their villages. During the same period, the 152 remaining members of the Arara tribe were given poisoned candy by jaguar poachers, and 118 died. The government closed down the Indian Protection Services, which had permitted these things to happen, but the atrocities continued. Anthropologist Anna Presland reported that army helicopters bombed the Arara in 1979. In Paraguay, anthropologists Mark Munzel and Miguel Chase Sardi reported that, until the late 1970s, the members of the Ache tribe were systematically hunted down, sometimes with the help of the Paraguayan army. The parents were often killed and the children sold into slavery.

In the 1980s, this treatment of the Amazonian natives received worldwide attention. Human-rights groups such as Survival International and the Anti-Slavery Society publicized the atrocities and worked to get the Latin American governments to stop them. The natives also began to organize themselves and issue official protests. In the early 1980s, the Yanomamo Indian Nation in Brazil presented a formal complaint to the Inter-

These Yanomamo Indians from northwest Brazil met in 1989 to protest against gold miners who had occupied their lands.

American Commission on Human Rights, claiming that the Brazilian government had violated their human and constitutional rights as well as several international conventions. Because of these pressures on the governments of the developing nations, it appears that native tribes are no longer being killed deliberately. Their rainforest homes, however, are still being destroyed, now even faster than before. If the destruction continues, those natives who have survived will eventually have no choice but to abandon their own culture and join the dominant culture of the people who govern their country.

When the natives try to give up their culture and assimilate into modern civilization, they run into problems. For one thing, they have never been exposed to many diseases or vaccinated against them. This means they have no immunity to diseases that are fairly common in modern civilization. Many natives die from such diseases as measles and flu. Also, their rainforest skills and knowledge are not valued by the dominant culture, and they are seldom given training in modern technology that would enable them to earn a decent living. Therefore, they enter society at the lowest level, usually as laborers, landless peasants, or even beggars. In one cruel twist of fate, the Conibo Indians in Bolivia ended up as laborers for the logging company that was destroying their rainforest home. Furthermore, the natives are used to either getting everything free from the rainforest or trading rainforest products for a few modern items. They are not accustomed to using money, and the companies that hire them take advantage of that inexperience. They force the natives to buy all their goods from the company store at high prices, and the natives often end up in debt that they can never pay back on their very low salaries. In the end, they often become dependent on government handouts. This dependence makes them depressed and childlike; in fact, in some countries they are legally minors with no rights.

Danger of extinction

Since 1492 when Christopher Columbus discovered the Americas, 95 percent of South America's native tribes have disappeared. The tribes that remain have become smaller. The Nambiquara tribe in Brazil maintained ten to fifteen thousand members for thousands of years. By 1985, there were only about five hundred. Many experts feel that most native cultures in Latin America are in danger of extinction because the dominant cultures are taking over the rainforests.

There is, however, one group of settlers in the Amazon who, like the natives, live and work in the

For hundreds of years, natives have lived in the rainforest without destroying the fragile ecosystem. Now, many native cultures and animals face the danger of extinction.

rainforest without destroying it and consider themselves rainforest people. They are the half million rubber tappers, workers called *seringueiros*, who gather latex from the wild rubber trees scattered throughout the rainforest. Rubber is made from the latex, a milky white juice in the trees. Early every morning, the tappers make a long, sloping cut in the bark halfway around each rubber tree. The latex slowly drips into a cup hung at the bottom of the cut. After the latex is collected from the cups, it hardens and is processed into rubber.

Rubber tappers have a long history in the rainforest. Ever since Columbus landed in the West Indies and found natives playing with rubber balls, the demand for rubber has grown. By the

A tapper (right) cuts into the bark of a rubber tree to obtain latex, a milky white juice that will slowly drip into a cup hung at the bottom of the incision (above).

nineteenth century, the demand had made rubber production a potentially very profitable business. Europeans and Americans went to Brazil hoping to make their fortunes by acquiring rainforest land and bringing in tappers at very low wages to harvest wild rubber. Many failed, but some succeeded for a time, despite the hardships. The town of Manaus on the Amazon River, two thousand miles from the river's mouth on the Atlantic Ocean, became one of the wealthiest cities in the world in the late nineteenth century. It had electric trams before Boston did and boasted an extremely elaborate opera house that attracted the best singers in the world. But the boom did not last. The hardships were too great. The Europeans and Americans got tired of fighting the hot, humid climate, the lack of modern conveniences, the uncertain market price for rubber, and the labor prob-

The da Silva family, shown here at their cabin in the western part of the Amazon jungle, earns their living by farming, raising a few animals, and tapping rubber.

lems from overworked and underpaid tappers, and they went home. Today Manaus is a tax-free zone that is becoming a center for electronics firms. The main reminder of the city's former grandeur is the opera house where local singers still give concerts.

Now, Brazilian landowners have monopolized the rubber industry. These rich landlords live in the big cities and hire managers to oversee their rubber production. But they are successful because their methods do not conflict with the rainforest's ecology. Instead of trying to grow rubber trees in plantations, they hire *seringueiros* to gather latex from the wild rubber trees. There are now about half a million people earning their living as tappers. These people of the rainforest suffer some of the same problems as the natives.

Manaus, Brazil, a port on the Amazon River. New buildings hover over the older buildings that line the waterfront.

Some independent *seringueiros* earn a decent living by collecting, processing, and selling rubber part of the year and Brazil nuts the rest of the year. But most work for huge companies that have no concern for their well-being. They are paid low wages for long hours of hard work and must depend on the company to ship all their food, clothing, and other supplies into the rainforest. When the supplies are slow in arriving, they must do without. When the supplies do arrive, the landowners price them very high so that the tappers end up in debt. This way, the landowners can prevent the tappers from becoming independent because they must stay with the company until the debt is paid off, and the debt keeps piling up.

Now the *seringueiros* face an even greater challenge from two fronts. On one side is the encroaching development that is destroying acres of rainforest. Since tappers, like the natives, rely on large tracts of undisturbed rainforest to survive, their careers are endangered. On the other side, the rubber industry in Brazil is beginning to turn to plantations again. The amount of rubber that can be harvested from wild trees is limited, and wild rubber is often full of debris, which lowers its selling price.

Rubber plantations in Malaysia and Indonesia

In the nineteenth century, rubber seeds from Brazil were taken to Malaysia where successful plantations were established. Malaysia and Indonesia now export over half the world's supply of rubber. Brazil exports only about 1 percent. Large plantations will help Brazil capture more of the world's market. But these plantations will not be in the hot, humid rainforest where they would be attacked by leaf blight. They will be in drier, cooler parts of the country where the blight cannot grow. One such plantation now uses approxi-

While collecting latex from trees, a tapper threads his way through the dense undergrowth.

mately fifteen hundred workers to produce about three thousand tons of rubber a year. In the rainforest, six thousand workers would be needed to produce that much. It is estimated that by 1991, 60 percent of the rubber Brazil produces will come from plantations outside the rainforests. If the plantations succeed, many *seringueiros* may find themselves out of work.

The *seringueiros* have built their own culture in the rainforest. It is their home, and they do not want to leave. They want their portion of the rainforest left undisturbed, and they want to be able to compete independently with other rubber producers. But like the natives, their culture may be doomed to extinction.

Scientists are concerned about both the *seringueiros* and the natives for obvious humanitarian reasons. But they have an additional concern. When these cultures die, the tribes' vast, ancient storehouse of knowledge about the rainforest will die with them. There is so much about the rainforest that experts do not yet know, and time is running out. With knowledge gained from the natives, experts hope to teach the new settlers in the rainforest how to use the natives' methods of conservation. They hope that the natives' knowledge of the complexity and fragility of the rainforest will help them understand what must be done to preserve as much of it as possible. If this fails and the rainforest is truly doomed, they at least want to find ways to save as many of the rainforest's resources as they can.

Native tribes have already taught the world about a great many of those resources. This knowledge has turned the rainforest into a virtual supermarket. People in developed countries like the United States cannot go through a day without using a least one product that originated in the rainforest.

Kaiapo Indians of Brazil, photographed in 1989 as they approached the small Amazon town of Altamira to protest the building of hydroelectric dams.

3

The World's Supermarket

MANY PEOPLE IN the world today owe their lives to the knowledge of the rainforest natives. Approximately one-fourth of all prescription drugs come from rainforest plants, and it was the people of the rainforest who first discovered how to use those plants. By trial and error, over thousands of years, the natives found plants that could cure heart disease, cancer, high blood pressure, diabetes, and many other human ailments. The Malaysian natives use as many twenty-five hundred plants for medicine; the natives of Java use perhaps two hundred; in the Amazon, the natives use more than one thousand. Ever since people from outside cultures first went to the rainforest, they have been learning the uses of these plants from the natives. Now scientists are studying these plants to adapt their uses to modern medicine.

Beneficial compounds

Rainforest plants are full of secondary compounds, chemicals that are not essential to growth but instead help the plants survive in their niche. Those compounds may be poisons that make the leaves deadly to eat, scents that attract pollinating insects, or colors that insects see as a warning of

(opposite page) Many drugs used today were derived from plants that originated in the rainforest.

45

danger. Other compounds fight off bacteria or promote rapid healing or growth. It is those chemicals that make the plants useful to medicine.

The Amazonian natives' cure for malaria was one of the first medical discoveries to reach the outside world. In the seventeenth century, malaria killed several million people a year all over the world, and it had been doing so for centuries. Father Calancha, a Spanish priest who lived in Peru, discovered in 1633 that the natives cured malaria with a powder made from the bark of the *cinchona* tree. But Father Calancha's discovery was ignored and considered as a hoax by both government and medical authorities in Europe. For years after that, various innovative scientists tried to introduce the cure to Europe, but it was not taken seriously until the early nineteenth century. Then, in 1820, two French doctors discovered the reason that the bark cured malaria. The bark contained a chemical that the doctors called quinine,

A marine on Guadalcanal during World War II sprays near camp for mosquitoes, which carried the malaria germ.

The bark of cinchona trees can be used to produce quinine, effective in combatting malaria.

after the native name for the bark, *quinaquina*, which means "bark of barks." But it was not until the end of the century that the Dutch finally succeeded in establishing thriving cinchona plantations on Java, thereby giving the world a reliable source of quinine. It is said that gin and tonic became the favorite drink of the British who lived and worked in the tropics because tonic contains quinine. They had reason to claim it was preventive medicine.

A new cure for malaria

Until 1944, quinine was the only treatment for malaria, and it saved millions of lives. But in 1942 during World War II, the Japanese captured Java, and the world's supply of quinine became dangerously short. In response, two U.S. scientists, William Doering and Robert Woodward, analyzed quinine's chemical formula and were able to duplicate the formula in a synthetic drug that was cheaper and often worked better than quinine. Since then, most of the world has used these synthetics, which include chloroquine and primaquine, to both prevent and treat malaria. At the

Dr. William E. Doering (left) and Dr. Robert B. Woodward (right) with a model of the quinine molecule. Doering and Woodward were the first to synthesize quinine.

During WWII, two officers look for mosquito larvae that they will analyze for signs of malaria.

same time, the mosquitoes that carry malaria have been eradicated from most of the developed nations. Malaria is now a problem only in tropical countries.

But that is not the end of the story. Those mosquitoes are rainforest creatures, and rainforest creatures have an amazing ability to survive by adapting to changes in their environment. After the synthetic drugs had been in use for less than forty years, some mosquitoes developed a resistance to them. This happened because the mosquitoes were drawing blood from people who were taking the drugs, and the drugs got into the mosquitoes' systems. Over time, their systems adapted to the presence of the drugs by developing different and stronger strains of malaria. In Thailand in 1960, 90 percent of the malaria victims who received chloroquine were cured. In 1982, only 20 percent were cured. The mosquitoes will continue to develop resistance to new drugs, and scientists fear that the need to find stronger drugs to combat the resistance will turn into a continuous cycle. But the mosquitoes have not developed resistance to natural quinine. In some places, quinine is again the primary drug used against malaria, and it is being used as a model to manufacture even stronger synthetic drugs. Scientists are again using the natives' knowledge of the rainforest, this time to seek other plants that may help in the fight against malaria.

Natives in Madagascar helped scientists discover a rainforest plant with equally marvelous powers. Natives used the leaves of the rosy periwinkle, a delicate plant with small white flowers, to treat diabetes. But, between 1960 and 1965, when scientists analyzed the chemistry of the plant, they found that six of its more than eighty different compounds could fight tumors. Now two of those six compounds, vincristine and vinblastine, are used to treat childhood leukemia, Hodgkin's disease, and other forms of cancer. In the 1960s, before those drugs were discovered, only 20 percent of the children with leukemia survived. Now 80 percent survive. There are, in fact, three thousand plants known to contain anticancer compounds, and more than two thousand of them live in the rainforest.

When the outside world first discovered curare, a sticky, black mixture of resins from two species of rainforest lianas, the Amazon natives were using it as poison on the tips of their arrows. Once the poison got into the animal it actually relaxed to death. Now curare is used during heart, abdominal, eye, and other delicate surgery to relax the muscles and make the surgeon's work easier. It is also used to treat multiple sclerosis, Parkinson's disease, and other muscle disorders.

Other rainforest derivatives

The list of medicines derived from the rainforest seems almost endless. Cortisone, used to treat arthritis and inflammation, and diosgenin, used in birth control pills, both come from a yam that

The Swallow-tail butterfly. Studies have shown that some butterflies may contain chemical compounds that fight cancer.

grows on the barbasco vine in Mexico. Rauwolfia, derived from the snakeroot plant of India, has been used as a tranquilizer by the natives for thousands of years. Now one of its compounds, reserpine, is used to treat high blood pressure, anxiety, and mental diseases. Picrotoxin, from the seeds of the Levant berry plant, restores breathing in people who have overdosed on drugs. All in all, as many as seven thousand medical substances are derived from plants. And scientists know there are many more waiting to be discovered.

They also know that a great deal of knowledge could be gained from studying rainforest animals. Those animals represent another potential storehouse of medicine, particularly the insects. For instance, studies have shown that some butterflies may contain compounds that fight cancer. There are millions of insects in the rainforest, many of them as yet undiscovered, and no one knows how many of them could provide a cure for a dreaded disease. Other animals need to be studied as well. Already, several species of Central American frogs are the source of a powerful anesthetic and muscle relaxant called tetrodotoxin.

Grocery store

From their first cup of coffee, tea, or hot chocolate in the morning to their midnight snack of oranges or ginger snaps, people all over the world enjoy food that originated in the rainforest. Coffee first came from the beans of a plant that lives in the understory of the Ethiopian rainforest in Africa. Tea is made from the leaves of a Southeast Asian plant, and chocolate comes from the beans of the Amazonian cacao plant. Oranges, papayas, bananas, mangoes, grapefruit, and pineapples are only a few of the fruits that were originally found growing wild in the rainforest. Ginger, black pepper, cloves, vanilla, cinnamon, nutmeg, and paprika are just a few of the spices that also originated in the rainforest. The long list of rainforest

A rice paddy in Bali, Indonesia. Rice is one of many foods that originated in the rainforest.

Other foods that originated in the rainforest include oranges, coffee, eggplant, ginger, bananas, and chocolate.

Coffee originated from the beans of a plant in the Ethiopian rainforest. Today, coffee is usually grown on plantations like this one.

foods includes corn, peanuts, sugarcane from which both white and brown sugar are made, rice, eggplant, tomatoes, and manioc, the source of tapioca.

Obviously, the world's supply of these foods no longer comes from the rainforest. It comes from farms and plantations. The original plants were taken out of the rainforest and domesticated. Domesticated plants are new varieties that are specifically bred to grow faster or yield more crops than the original plant. But this breeding gradually changes the plant's genetic structure. As the new varieties become increasingly different from the original rainforest plant, they lose more and more of their protective compounds. That makes them increasingly less resistant to diseases and insects. Since only one food crop is grown on a plantation instead of a variety of crops, diseases and insect pests spread rapidly once they start.

Vulnerability to disease is a particular problem when it involves the few basic crops that feed most of the world's population. About two dozen crops, including soybeans, peanuts, coconuts, manioc, and potatoes, supply the majority of protein and calories consumed by the world's population. Over half of the world's food comes from just three crops—rice, wheat, and corn, or, as it is called in some parts of the world, maize. When a major disease strikes these crops, it is a disaster for the people who depend on them. The Irish potato famine from 1845 to 1847 is a well-known example of such a crop failure. Potatoes were then the main food source in Ireland. By the time the potato blight that killed the potatoes had run its course, 750,000 Irish were dead of starvation, and millions more had left the country.

Preventing disaster

The best way to prevent such a disaster is to go back to the original rainforest plants. They have maintained their resistance to disease. Every five to fifteen years, crop breeders need to mix the genes of the wild plants with the genes of the domesticated plants to strengthen the crops. In the last fifty years or so, genes from wild rainforest plants have been used to save a number of important crops, including coffee, sugarcane, cacao, manioc, and bananas.

The rainforest can also help save domesticated crops from insects. In order to protect themselves against the millions of insects in their ecosystem, rainforest plants contain a number of different chemicals that work as natural insecticides. Not only do these work well but they are less toxic to humans and animals than the synthetic insecticides normally used on crops. Scientists are working to process those natural chemicals for commercial use and have already succeeded with

A sugar mill borders this cane field in Honolulu, Hawaii. Sugarcane originated in the rainforest.

a few. For example, the root of a liana called derris is used by the rainforest tribes of Southeast Asia as poison on their arrows. Derris root contains a chemical called rotenone that is used today to kill insects on crops.

The complexity of the rainforest has even provided farmers with an alternative means of getting rid of pests. Many insects in the rainforest eat other insects. So a species of insect that eats the pest can be captured in the rainforest and released in the fields. This is called biological pest control. Citrus farmers in Florida have imported

Settlers and natives continue to build roads into the forest so that they can collect the abundant wood, plants, and animals.

three species of wasps to eat pests. In 1910, sugarcane plantations in Hawaii were losing close to one million dollars a year because the sugarcane beetle borer was ruining their crops. Then the tachinid fly, a parasite that kills the beetle, was discovered in the rainforests of New Guinea. It was brought to Hawaii and saved the sugarcane crops.

New food crops

People have been growing the same basic food crops for thousands of years. This is true not because they are necessarily the best food crops but because they are traditional. Most of the crops were selected ten thousand years ago by the first farmers who found them the most convenient crops to grow. The rainforest is full of plants that may be a better source of protein, or better tasting, or easier, faster, and cheaper to grow. These include beans (a valuable source of protein), vegetables, and fruits.

For instance, the world has just begun to discover the wide variety of tropical fruits. Some, like the kiwi—which was unknown in the United States until the 1970s—have now become common. Although grocery stores in the United States sell a much wider variety of tropical fruits than they did even ten years ago, there are many more waiting to be enjoyed. The rainforest contains more than two thousand different fruits, and only a few dozen are well-known. Many of the lesser-known ones are just as tasty and nutritious and could become just as popular. Fruits such as pummelo, soursop, naranjilla, rambutan, starfruit, and mangosteen may seem strange now, but so were tomatoes when they were first introduced to the outside world. In fact, the tomato, which is a fruit, was first grown as an ornamental plant in Europe because it was thought to be poisonous.

The rainforest is a vast supplier of much more

than medicine and food. Every time people chew gum, drive a car, go jogging, or wash their hair, they are using products derived from the rainforest. The rainforest harvest includes oils, gums, resins, dyes, waxes, latex, shellac, perfumes, fibers, glues, fats, alcohols, acids, and disinfectants. This harvest is big business for the rainforest countries. It provides jobs for the poor, and the countries earn millions of dollars every year by exporting the goods.

Lumber from tropical rainforest trees is the largest export. As the amount of forest left in the rest of the world decreases, the developed countries place more and more restrictions on lumbering in their own forests. But demand for lumber remains high in developed countries, and the rainforest countries are glad to cut down their trees to supply that demand. The more exotic wood is made into furniture. Mahogany chairs and tables, teak desks, and rosewood paneling are considered well worth the very high prices. Less exotic lumber is needed for building and for pulp to make paper. More than half of the exported

Lumber is just one of the rainforest exports. Here, a hydraulic lift loads a truck bound for a lumber mill.

rainforest lumber goes to Japan, with Europe in second place, and the United States in third.

The Southeast Asian rainforests have been logged more heavily than any others. Many of their canopy trees have been cut down for lumber. This has left large areas of secondary rainforest. Rattan, a liana that is actually the spiny stem of various palm trees, grows well in secondary

In Brazil, workmen join hands around the trunk of a tree to show its giant circumference.

rainforests. It is now Southeast Asia's second most valuable export. These long, ropy lianas are used to make a wide variety of things, including wicker furniture. Since rattan vines are scattered throughout the rainforest and have not yet been grown successfully on plantations, it requires a great deal of labor to harvest them. This provides jobs for many people. These people know how much money can be made from processing the rattan and have begun to make the chairs, baskets, ropes, and other rattan products themselves.

Oils from the rainforest

Essential oils are another important export from the rainforest. The United States imports oils worth more than $100 million every year. Essential, in this case, does not mean necessary: it means the oils have an essence, or scent, that comes from a group of compounds called terpenoids. Essential oils are used to manufacture perfumes, cosmetics, shampoos, and foods. They are what we smell in coffee, incense, and curry. A wide variety of plants contain these oils—plants like citronella, sandalwood, patchouli, camphor, ginger, cinnamon, nutmeg, and clove. Some are rare and hard to harvest and, therefore, very expensive. The oil of the ylang-ylang tree, highly prized by French perfume makers, comes from the flowers. They must be picked early every morning before the sun's heat evaporates the delicate oil. Oil from distilled wood chips of the sandalwood tree has been used in perfume for four thousand years. Oils are present everywhere in plants, in the flowers, leaves, bark, seeds, and roots. As scientists explore the rainforest and learn more about its plants, the potential for discovering new oils of all kinds is extremely promising.

Rattan for wicker furniture (below) is made from the lianas that grow on palm trees (above).

Some scientists are now exploring the possibility of using oils from the rainforest to replace petroleum as a source of fuel. The petroleum reserves in the world are being depleted while, at

the same time, the demand for them is rising. Being able to run our cars and heat our houses with plant materials would decrease U.S. dependency on the oil-producing countries of the Middle East.

One promising oil, a sap called liquid balsam, has been tapped from copaiba trees in the Amazon for years and exported for use in medicine and perfume. The natives drill a small hole in the trunk and then plug the hole. They return to the tree twice a year, remove the plug, and drain out up to twenty quarts of sap. In 1979, American chemist Melvin Calvin discovered that the sap is very similar to diesel fuel. He poured the sap directly into the tank of a diesel truck, and it ran. Scientists have since planted several copaiba plantations to experiment with liquid balsam.

The petroleum nut tree in the Philippines is another potential source of fuel. The nuts are so

A Brazilian native adapts North American tools to harvest timber.

flammable when they are first picked that they can be lit with a match. For many years, the natives have used oil from the nuts to fuel their lamps. The Japanese actually used it to run their tanks during World War II. This nut tree does not need as much rain as many other rainforest trees, so it might make a good plantation tree in secondary rainforests and drier parts of the tropics. Twice a year, each tree grows enough nuts to produce almost twelve gallons of oil. If people in the tropics planted six trees on their land, they could produce enough fuel for their own home use.

The existence of all these products, however, depends on the survival of the rainforest. If the rainforest is destroyed, most of its plants and animals will become extinct. Even now, scientists estimate that one to six species is lost forever every hour. No one knows how many species are becoming extinct before they are even discovered and named. The chances of finding a new plant that cures AIDS, a new food crop, a fuel that does not cause pollution, or a better insecticide get slimmer and slimmer every day. When the rainforest is gone, even the crops already grown on farms and plantations and the animals preserved in zoos will suffer. There may be no wild genes left to strengthen their resistance against disease and insects. And when the trees are gone, the developing countries will no longer be able to strengthen their economies through the export of rainforest products.

But all these material products, including those not yet discovered, are only a small portion of the rainforest's value to the world. There are other benefits that are even less understood and possibly even more important. They are the ones it is impossible to put a price on.

4

Priceless Contributions

BECAUSE THERE IS still a great deal scientists do not understand about the rainforest, the discovery of new knowledge often changes their theories. Until quite recently, for example, many scientists believed that the rainforests produced much of the earth's oxygen. They were afraid that if the rainforests were destroyed, the supply of oxygen would become dangerously low, threatening the survival of all human and animal life on the planet. Now scientists agree that the rainforest does not contribute any oxygen to the earth's supply. The rainforest, as a self-sustaining system, uses all the oxygen it produces as energy to decompose its living soil.

But while scientists were sighing in relief over this discovery, they found another potentially devastating effect of deforestation, or the destruction of forests. According to rainforest expert Norman Myers, many scientists think that rainforests help stabilize the earth's climate by absorbing much of the solar radiation, or heat, from the sun's rays. When rainforests are destroyed, the bare land left behind reflects more solar radiation back into the earth's atmosphere. This is called the albedo effect. It is most obvious in the

(opposite page) Many scientists now think that destruction of the rainforests may affect world climate.

63

Just as glass traps the heat inside of a greenhouse, gases from pollution (above) and deforestation trap the sun's heat in the earth's atmosphere (right).

glare on snow and desert sand. Some experts think that, as deforestation increases, the resulting increase in the reflection of radiation could affect wind currents, temperature, and rainfall in distant countries. Other experts, including Catherine Caufield, think that an increase in the albedo effect will change the climate locally in the rainforest areas, making the days hotter and the nights colder. Experts do not yet have any conclusive scientific proof that an increased albedo effect from deforestation affects climate. But if it does, the outlook is not good because rainforests are now disappearing at a rate of between forty and fifty million acres a year.

The greenhouse effect

But that is only the beginning of deforestation's effect on world climate. The rainforest is full of new settlers who burn large quantities of trees and vegetation to clear fields for crops. Most scientists feel the burning has contributed to

the greenhouse effect, which is the gradual but increasingly greater rise in the temperature of the earth's surface. Over the last one hundred years, the earth's average temperature has risen one degree Fahrenheit. Half of that increase has been since 1965. Some scientists think the temperature will rise another three to eight degrees by the year 2050. The name of this phenomenon comes from the fact that after the sun's rays enter a greenhouse, the glass traps the heat inside, keeping the greenhouse warm. In a similar way, when the sun's heat is reflected off the earth back into space, some of it is trapped in the gases in the earth's atmosphere. This trapped heat warms the earth. The more gases there are in the atmosphere, the more trapped heat there will be.

The greenhouse effect is a controversial topic. The majority of scientists think the greenhouse effect exists, but not all agree. Some, including Kenneth E.F. Watt, a professor of environmental studies, claim that there has been no measurable global warming. Others, including S. Fred Singer, a geophysicist, believe the greenhouse effect exists but claim the warming poses no danger because it will be balanced by nature, perhaps by an increase in heat-reflecting clouds.

The only thing all experts agree on is that the carbon dioxide in the atmosphere is increasing and that, in some way, this will have a major effect on every person in the world. Slowing down or halting deforestation is one way to help decrease the amount of carbon dioxide released into the atmosphere.

Loss of weather protection

Deforestation also affects the environment in other ways. Hundreds, sometimes hundreds of thousands, of people in the tropics are killed each year by cyclones, which are also called typhoons

The clearing of trees in the Amazon region of Brazil often leaves behind desert-like conditions. International pressure is mounting on Brazil to preserve its fast-disappearing rainforests.

Hurricane Flora in Cuba, 1963. Primary rainforests help to lessen the destruction of hurricanes by absorbing much of the rain and wind.

and hurricanes. These storms originate over the ocean, and when they hit land, they bring high winds, torrential rain, and gigantic tidal waves. Primary rainforests help to decrease the destructive power of the storms by absorbing the rain and buffering the environment from the wind. On islands and coastal areas where rainforests have been destroyed, loss of human life and damage to the environment is now much greater.

Rainforests prevent soil erosion by trapping the soil in their root mats. In areas where the rainforest has been destroyed, the effects of soil erosion have been devastating. When the topsoil erodes off a cleared plot of rainforest, the land is worthless. It cannot be farmed, and the rainforest can never grow back. But there are other consequences as well. What is happening to the Panama

Canal is a good example. Half of the canal consists of two man-made lakes that were surrounded by rainforest in 1950. Deforestation has occurred at such a rapid rate since then that experts predict all primary rainforest in the area will be gone by the year 2000. When it rains on the cleared areas, the rain erodes the soil and carries it into the lakes, causing what is known as siltation. This means that the lakes are slowly beginning to fill up with silt, a fine, loose soil. Some experts say that 40 percent of the lakes will be filled with silt by the year 2000. Eventually, if this continues, the canal will become useless to large ships. At times, it already is. As early as 1977, the siltation and a bad drought combined to drop the water level so low that some cargo ships could not get through. They had to go all the way around Cape Horn at the tip of South America.

Changes in streams and rivers

Siltation is also a problem in rivers and streams. It kills the fish, an important source of protein for people in developing countries. It clogs farmers' irrigation canals, and the water floods onto the fields, dropping the silt on the crops and smothering them. And it slows down the supply of water from the rainforest. An undisturbed rainforest provides not only itself but also other parts of the rainforest countries with water. By releasing water slowly, the rainforest delivers a steady supply of clear, clean water to rivers and streams. Eventually, the water trickles into wells, springs, and reservoirs. Far from the rainforest, it is used for drinking water by people who live in cities and for irrigating fields on farms in drier parts of the country.

Because the rainforest is a giant sponge that absorbs vast amounts of rain, it prevents floods. Where the rainforests have been destroyed, great

Brazilian river workers cut jute along the banks of the Amazon. Jute, used to make burlap and twine, is one of the most important crops in the Amazon area.

amounts of water are lost in floods. Because the water washes away so quickly, the soil cannot absorb it. In addition, flooding water carries away huge quantities of topsoil and deposits it as silt in lakes, rivers, and reservoirs. Worst of all, in some deforested areas, floods kill many people every year. For hundreds of years in Bangladesh near India, people have lived on the floodplain where the Ganges River flows into the Bay of Bengal. When rainforests covered the foothills of the Himalaya Mountains to the north, the flooding of the Ganges was usually predictable and restricted, and the damage could be controlled. But now those rainforests are largely gone, and during the rainy season, raging floods go out of control and kill hundreds of people every year. Those that live lose their homes, crops, and livestock.

A scientific laboratory

The rainforest's contribution to the world's environment has received considerable publicity because deforestation means potential disaster for people everywhere. But there are other contribu-

The Sumatran Orangutan is endangered by rainforest destruction.

The Hercules beetle, a native of Central and South America. Many species of insects are becoming extinct before they have even been discovered.

tions that some scientists are very concerned about. They see the rainforest as a gigantic scientific laboratory full of undiscovered knowledge. As a complex ecosystem filled with mystery and life, the rainforest can help increase their knowledge in all the earth sciences. As an ancient system of constantly evolving organisms, the rainforest may answer questions about the origins of life and intelligence and the struggle for survival. And it can teach scientists techniques to improve agriculture, forestry, animal husbandry, and medicine. Since so little is known about the rainforest, scientists can only guess at the amount of knowledge that will remain hidden if the rainforests are destroyed, but they are certain the loss would be tremendous.

Scientists want to save this fascinating, fragile laboratory, but some fear it is too late, that people will not act fast enough. In that case, they hope the destruction of the rainforest can be slowed down long enough to allow them to gather as much information as possible.

The extinction of rainforest animals also has scientists concerned. Never before in history has the earth been threatened with the extinction of so many species in such a short span of time. Not only are many species, mostly insects, becoming extinct before they have even been discovered,

Scientists can learn many things from studying the great variety of life in the rainforest.

A drawing illustrates the diversity of life in the rainforest. If current trends in deforestation continue, many species will become extinct.

but many of the animals that people have grown to appreciate now appear doomed in the wild. The world would be a less interesting place without the dignity of the jaguar, the agile antics of the woolly spotted monkey, or the graceful flight of the white Bali mynah bird. Like the tiger, mountain gorilla, bird of paradise, Asian rhinoceros, tapir, orangutan, lemur, forest elephant, okapi, and golden lion tamarin (monkey), they are presently in danger of extinction.

The rainforest creatures are not the only animals that are being affected by deforestation. At certain times of the year, the rainforest is home to numerous species of birds that live in North America. Warblers, orioles, thrushes, and other North American birds migrate south to the rainforests of Latin America every winter. In fact, more than one-third of North American birds join that migration. No one is sure what effect deforestation will have on migrating birds. But their survival may depend on the rainforest.

There is another contribution the rainforests make that is neither scientific nor necessary for human survival, but some people think it is just as important. That is the rainforest's aesthetic value, the sheer wonder of its beauty and abundant life, its complexity and uniqueness. The wonder of outer space drove nations to spend millions of dollars on space programs, but only a handful of people may ever get to see the beauty of other planets and stars at close range. If the rainforest is preserved, it can be enjoyed by a much larger percentage of the world's population.

5

Reasons for Deforestation

THE RAINFORESTS ARE so valuable and contribute so much to the world that their destruction may seem totally irresponsible. But the truth is that there are some compelling reasons for deforestation. The main one is economic. The developing nations that own the rainforests are poor. They see the rainforest as a rich natural resource that can be exploited for money. The rainforests offer a way to escape grinding poverty. Unfortunately, because their economic problems are so pressing, these countries have rushed into quick solutions instead of forming long-range plans. Such planning would allow exploitation of the rainforest's resources without destroying it. The quick solutions, such as extensive deforestation for logging and farming, are resulting in widespread destruction. Sometimes this is because the government underestimates the fragility of the rainforest. Sometimes rainforest development projects simply get too big or too complex to manage properly. Corruption and complacency in the government, the greed of wealthy landowners, and the poverty of new settlers also play a part. Rainforest destruction is also due to the economic policies of the developed nations.

(opposite page) The people of the developing nations that own the rainforests are threatened with hunger and unemployment. Here, a mother and four children wait for emergency food relief.

73

A farmer in Brazil's Amazon region clears debris after burning fifty acres of land to clear room for crops.

The rainforest countries have borrowed billions of dollars from the developed nations over the years. Very often, developing countries cannot afford to pay back this foreign debt, but they do have to pay the annual interest charged by the lending governments. Brazil, for instance, spends 40 percent of the money it earns on exports just to pay the yearly interest on its foreign debt, which totals more than $100 billion. Since most of Brazil's exports come from the rainforest, the only way it can get this money every year is to get the resources out of the rainforest as quickly as possible. That allows no time for conservation. And paying just the interest does not reduce the amount of debt. When the rainforest countries have asked for more time to pay back the debt, the developed nations have agreed, but only if certain conditions are met. One of those conditions is that the countries reduce their government spending. Often the first things to go are the agencies that manage and create policies for the environment and the natural resources.

A new frontier

To give them credit, the governments in the developing countries did not set out to destroy the rainforests; they wanted to develop them. They view the rainforest as a new frontier waiting to be developed, just as Americans viewed the West in the nineteenth century. The major resource in that frontier is the land the rainforest sits on. The land itself is so valuable because of the other major reason for deforestation: rapid population growth. The populations of the developing nations are expected to double by the year 2010. Brazil is a good example of what is happening as a result of this population growth.

Brazil is a large country, but it does not have enough cleared land for all its people, the majority of whom live in wretched poverty. Many of those people live in the cities, where they hope to find work, but most live in the countryside. Even

Rainforest settlers and natives continue to build damaging roads into the rainforest so that they can access lumber-rich land and plant crops.

The Trans-Amazon highway (above) strikes through the heart of Brazil's Amazon jungles. The highway spans 3,350 miles.

there, as much as 50 to 90 percent of the people do not legally own land. Without land, they cannot grow the food they need to survive. Of course, the land shortage is largely due to the fact that most of the land in Brazil and in the other Latin American countries is owned by wealthy landlords. The poor who want to own farmland must move where land is still available. Most of them end up in the rainforest.

The government encourages this migration for two main reasons. It relieves the poverty and crowded conditions in other parts of the country, and it helps colonize, or bring civilization to, the unpopulated parts of the country. Colonization is important because it helps control the often rebellious native tribes and protects the country's territory from invasion by bringing the newly settled areas under more government control.

The governments of all developing nations en-

Brazil and the Trans-Amazon Highway

Amazon Rainforest

Source: The Environmentalist

courage colonization by building roads into the rainforest. In fact, the roads serve a number of purposes. In countries rich in natural resources such as oil and gold, that are difficult to reach, roads encourage exploration to discover new deposits. In areas that are experiencing political turmoil, as many developing nations do from time to time, roads allow movements of military troops to patrol trouble spots and protect borders. In the lumber-rich rainforest countries, roads increase exports by opening up new areas to logging companies. And they bring streams of settlers. Roads, therefore, not only make it possible for people to damage the ecosystem, but they destroy large areas of the fragile rainforest themselves. The damage extends beyond the areas cleared for the roads themselves

The clearings made for the roads change the ecosystem for hundreds of feet on either side by letting in sunlight, disturbing water drainage and absorption, and bisecting the animals' territories. They force native tribes off their traditional land. Because of poor planning, many roads occasionally flood, isolating the settlers and preventing them from getting their crops to market. Others are built through areas where there is a high incidence of tropical diseases like malaria. Both the settlers and the natives suffer from the subsequent spread of those diseases.

Poachers

The roads also bring another danger into the rainforest—poachers. They do not contribute to deforestation, but poachers do endanger the survival of many rainforest species. While these poachers are only trying to earn a living in the most profitable way available to them, they cause destruction nonetheless. Even though trade in endangered animals is now illegal in most areas of the world, a profitable market still exists in other parts. Forest elephants are still killed for the ivory in their tusks. Gorillas are slaughtered so their heads can be mounted and their hands made into ashtrays for souvenirs. Leopard skins, tortoise-shells, and rhinoceros horns all contribute to the poacher's income. Feathers from the rainforest's colorful birds are valuable, and the birds them-selves sell for thousands of dollars on the illegal market. Some poachers make a living just selling rare butterflies. Many countries try to stop poach-ing, even to the point of having their game war-dens shoot poachers on sight, but funds to pro-vide the necessary protection are low and the rainforest is huge. When the poachers are caught, more often than not the animals are already dead.

Another way the Brazilian government encour-ages colonization is by offering the settlers legal ownership to some land, technical farming assis-tance, and money if they are willing to relocate. Unfortunately, this expensive program is poorly planned and managed. Many settlers never re-ceive the technical assistance they were promised. And for every family that is actually settled legally under the program, many more follow the roads into the rainforest and illegally squat on the land.

Ignorance of the rainforest ecology

All any of these settlers want is to grow enough food to feed themselves, plus some sur-plus crops they can sell to get money for other necessary items. Many of them fail to achieve this because the new settlers do not understand the rainforest ecology.

For example, many settlers cannot pick a good place to clear a field. They tend to pick places where the rainforest trees are the biggest, think-ing that means the soil is more fertile. But the

A burnt section of rainforest on Africa's Ivory Coast awaits planting. Experts estimate that slash-and-burn farming is the number one cause of worldwide rainforest destruction.

In Africa, a pair of young elephants sleep in the shade of their elders. Elephants are still killed for their ivory tusks.

rainforest natives know that places where the trees have thin trunks often have the best soil. In addition, the new settlers use a destructive farming technique that involves slashing and burning large areas of vegetation. It is the primary cause of deforestation. Experts estimate that slash-and-burn farming accounts for somewhere between 60 and 70 percent of worldwide rainforest destruction each year.

Like shifting cultivators, slash-and-burn farmers begin by cutting down and burning the primary rainforest to clear fields, but that is where the similarity ends. The settlers do not plant a wide variety of crops, nor do they recycle the fields. They must constantly fight erosion, weeds, insect pests, and plant diseases. In two or three years, when the field is infertile, it is abandoned, and another field is cleared out of either primary or secondary rainforest, and then another and another. Many of these abandoned fields are so badly eroded that the rainforest cannot reclaim them. They become wasteland, and the settlers have no choice but to leave. In 1982, a highway was built through the Brazilian state of Rondonia. The people who were settled there cleared almost thirty-five thousand square miles of rainforest. Within four years, most of the original settlers had given up and moved on.

The logging industry

After slash-and-burn farming, the main cause of deforestation is logging. It accounts for about 15 percent of the destruction worldwide, and this figure is increasing every year. Until the 1960s, logging was usually done by hand on a small scale, and little damage was done to the rainforest. Then the increasing demand for lumber from the developed nations and the introduction of

An African native cuts down a tree with a hand saw. Before the introduction of electric logging equipment, loggers did little damage to the rainforest.

bulldozers, chain saws, log-hauling vehicles, and roads turned logging into big business. Logging companies now lease the right to log a certain area from the private owners or the government on a short-term basis. They do not own the land and are not concerned about conserving it. They are interested only in logging the most valuable trees as quickly as possible.

Logging companies do not usually cut down all the trees. They practice what is called selective logging by harvesting only the best and largest lumber trees, which equals from 5 to 40 percent of the total. Since each acre of rainforest contains only a few of those trees, the rainforest might be able to survive this loss if it were the only destruction the logging companies did. But the damage is far more extensive than this. Experts estimate that felling one tree can destroy seventeen other trees. When the cut trees fall, the intertwined lianas pull down many young trees with them. Many seedlings are crushed when the logs are hauled out. The heavy machinery compacts the earth, interrupting water drainage and destroying the root mat that is necessary to the rainforest's fragile closed system. In the end, up to 70 percent of the rainforest in a logging area is destroyed for the sake of a few trees.

Logged trees as a fuel source

The logged trees are meant mostly for export, but trees from the rainforest are also used by the local people for fuel. Most people in the developing countries do not have electricity or natural gas. They cook mainly over wood fires. Norman Myers and other experts believe that only a small percentage of the primary rainforest is cut down every year for household fuel, but no one really knows for sure. Most firewood is probably taken from secondary forest and from logged areas,

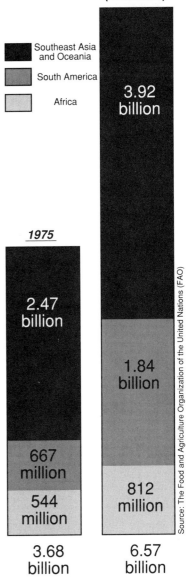

Tropical Hardwood Cut for Commercial Use
Amounts are in cubic feet

Source: The Food and Agriculture Organization of the United Nations (FAO)

Because many people in developing countries do not have electricity, they rely on wood for household fuel. Experts believe that each person uses between half a ton and one ton of firewood every year.

since it is easier to gather dead wood from the rainforest floor than to chop down trees. But each person uses between half a ton and one ton of firewood every year. As the population steadily increases, so will the need for fuel. That need means more trouble for the rainforest.

Other fuel needs are also a problem. In Brazil, for instance, the iron, brick, and cement industries burn charcoal in their ovens to reduce the amount of money spent on importing coal. The charcoal is often made from rainforest trees. One acre of rainforest provides from twenty-five to thirty tons of charcoal, but an iron factory can burn that much in just two hours. In this way, Brazil's growing industries are built at the expense of its rainforest.

The destruction continues even after the loggers have gone. Many animals lose their niches, and species that depend on the lost trees cannot survive. The bare areas left behind erode and undermine tree roots, and more trees fall. The erosion causes siltation in rivers. And many times, farmers and ranchers take advantage of the partial clearing because it saves them work. They finish the destruction by burning the logged areas for crop fields and cattle pastures.

Ranchers cause deforestation

In fact, so many ranchers have come to the rainforest that ranchers are the third largest cause of rainforest destruction. In Central America, it is the main cause. In all Latin American countries, cattle ranchers occupy far more rainforest land than farmers. Besides taking over logged land and farmland deserted by its owners, they buy big areas of land cheaply and hire workers for very low wages to slash and burn the rainforest and plant grass. An even cheaper way to clear the land they buy is to allow farmers to do it for them. The ranchers do not pay the farmers but give them the right to grow and harvest one food crop on the land before they plant it with grass and move on.

In Central America, well over one-quarter of the rainforest has been cleared for cattle pasture since 1960. In Costa Rica, for example, pastures occupy over one-third of the country. Because the ranchers acquire the rainforest land very cheaply, the cost of raising cattle is low. That means they can sell the beef they export cheaply. About half of it is bought by the United States, where it is used in cheap hamburgers, hot dogs, and pet food. Many ranches are simply hobbies for their rich owners who live in the cities and are interested only in making a profit. They do not care about increasing their production or conserving the land. They do not even care that the land is unsuitable for ranching.

When their pastures are ruined, the ranchers leave them to erode into barren wasteland and move on to turn another area of rainforest into grazing land. They see this as development, not destruction. They feel the rainforest is unproductive land. To them, it is empty, worthless wilder-

Ranchers use logged-out jungles as cattle pastures. Even though the land is unsuitable for ranching, it is cheap and guarantees the ranchers a substantial profit.

ness. By converting it into grassland, ranchers believe they are doing something beneficial.

Since ranchers can acquire huge areas of rainforest very cheaply, they can make a profit by reselling part of the land. In most Latin American countries, the only way to establish legal ownership of land is to prove it is being used. The easiest way to do that is to clear it. But only half of it has to be cleared. Some greedy ranchers clear half their land and then sell the other half at a profit. The buyer clears half of that and sells the remaining half at a profit. And so it goes until almost all the rainforest on the original tract of land is gone. If gold or diamonds are discovered on the land, the ranchers can make a huge profit, because the price of the land will skyrocket. The mining projects that follow that discovery are another cause of rainforest destruction.

Destruction of the rainforest continues as miners use bulldozers to clear land in Brazil.

The Amazon and other rainforest areas often have rich deposits of aluminum, tin, copper, uranium, iron, and other minerals, as well as gold and diamonds. Before the 1960s, mining on a small scale had gone on in the rainforest for many years with no ill effects. Since then, however, it has become big business, and now many of the mines are run by big mining companies. The mines themselves do not normally destroy large areas of rainforest. However, the mining operations are damaging to the fragile ecosystem. High-pressure water is used to dig the pits and extract the ore and causes erosion. In Malaysia in 1980, landslides started by copper mining covered thirty-seven hundred acres of rice paddies with as much as twelve inches of mud. Six hundred and twenty families had to be relocated. The water used to extract the ore turns the mining pits into muddy ponds where mosquitoes breed, making malaria a serious problem in mining areas. But the major problem is caused by the poisonous mercury used to remove the impurities from gold. The mercury washes into the rivers, endangers the ecosystem, kills the fish, and makes the water unfit for human use.

Brazilian prospectors hunt for gold. Since the 1960s, mining has become big business in the Amazon and other rainforest areas.

Gold prospectors

The problem in Brazil has gotten worse in the last twenty years because the rainforest has been invaded by prospectors hoping to make their fortunes. Whenever gold is discovered, the rush is on. For instance, since 1987, more than forty thousand hopeful prospectors have overrun the Roraima territory in northwestern Brazil. These transient gold miners are called *garimpeiros*. They mine illegally, so there are no controls on their operations, and they have built hundreds of illegal airstrips in the rainforest. Their invasion has endangered the survival of the natives of Roraima, the Yanomamo Indians, one of the last independent native tribes in Brazil. Gold miners have introduced new diseases to the natives and poisoned their rivers with mercury. As a result, violence has broken out between the natives and the *garimpeiros*. Missionaries in the region estimate that 20 percent of the nine thousand Yanomami have died as a result of these problems.

A source of electricity

Hydroelectric dams that generate power from water are often associated with mining projects and other industries that need the power they produce to run their operations. The governments of the developing countries hire huge, international corporations to build these dams as part of the countries' development schemes. Each dam creates a lake, or reservoir, that floods hundreds of square miles of primary rainforest. But the electricity these dams produce is a more efficient energy supply than wood or charcoal. Most developing countries believe a reliable source of electricity is an important step in their economic development. For one thing, having their own source of energy will save part of the millions of dollars spent on importing oil. As long as enough of the countries' primary rainforest is left intact, it is a reliable source of hydroelectric power. In the Amazon, for instance, there are more than one thousand rivers and streams. The water flowing through them every day accounts for one-fifth of all the fresh water on earth. The daily energy in that water is equivalent to the energy from five million barrels of oil. On paper, dams seem to be a perfect form of rainforest development, but, as with many other projects in the rainforest, they often end up causing more problems than they solve.

The companies that build the dams do not want

Because of unregulated expansion of gold mining in Brazil, the Yanomamo Indians are threatened with extinction. Here, chiefs from seventy-six tribes dance before the Congress building, chanting in defense of the vanishing tribe.

to take the time and expense to remove the trees before they flood the rainforest. As the drowned trees decompose under the water, they produce gases. Some of those gases stink, some deplete the oxygen supply in the water, some make the water very acidic, and some are poisonous. The smell bothers people many miles downwind, and the workers at the dam often have to wear gas masks. The acid corrodes the dam's metal equipment, requiring millions of dollars' worth of repairs and replacements. The lack of oxygen in the water kills many fish and stuns other fish as far away as fifty miles downstream. Nutrients from the decomposing trees produce a floating garden of water hyacinths, ferns, and other waterweeds on hundreds of square miles of the reservoirs. The plants get caught in the dam's machinery,

Much of the Ivory Coast in Africa is covered with dense rainforest. However, logging, ranching, and mining operations have taken their toll on the once-lush landscape.

compounding the damage from the acid. They also kill most of the other plants in the reservoir by absorbing the nutrients and blocking out the sun. That kills more fish because they depend on the other plants for food. On top of all that, malaria-carrying mosquitoes breed in the water.

After the dams are built, settlers come up the roads and begin to farm around them. When the surrounding area is cleared, the land begins to erode. The reservoirs often fill up with silt, making the dams useless. In some areas, the runoff of water from cleared land has actually smashed the dams. The Anchicaya Reservoir in Colombia lasted only fifteen years before it was almost completely filled with silt. Every time this happens, hundreds more acres of rainforest must be flooded to build new dams.

No matter what the reason for the damage done to the rainforest, the result is the same. The rainforests are disappearing at a rapid rate. Somewhere between forty and fifty million acres are being destroyed each year. If that rate of destruction continues, the primary rainforests will all disappear in the first quarter of the next century.

Deforestation causes droughts in Ethiopia

The rainforest countries' attempts to develop their economies may backfire if they do not halt the destruction. Without the rainforest, much of the land could become desert. This has already happened in Ethiopia, where the local climate has been seriously affected by deforestation for farming. When the rainforests were destroyed, the rain and runoff water they provided to the farmers ceased. This caused serious droughts. During droughts, crops cannot grow on the mostly infertile soil, and thousands of people starve to death, despite relief efforts from countries around the world. By cutting down the rainforest as a quick

A parched field in Ethiopia illustrates the serious effects of deforestation, which turned much of the Ethiopian rainforest to desert.

solution to creating farmland, the Ethiopians destroyed not only the rainforest but also their long-term farming opportunities.

The problem, of course, is finding ways to save the rainforest that also allow the countries to develop and prosper. That will take long-term planning, government control, enforcement of laws, and, most of all, money.

6

Saving the Rainforest

THE DEVELOPING NATIONS that own the rainforests have the right to decide how to use them. Blaming them for the destruction of the rainforests will not solve the problems, nor will it gain their cooperation in saving them. As those nations point out, Americans did the same thing when we were developing our own country. We killed our native Indians and drove them off their land. We cut down our forests for pastures and fields. We built dams, mined, hunted animal species almost to extinction, and generally ignored the effects of development on the environment. And now we are asking other countries to stop developing because their deforestation will affect the rest of the world. It is no wonder they are defensive about how they use their rainforests.

A global problem

Still, the rainforest countries are concerned about deforestation. Many of them have taken steps to try to conserve their rainforests and lessen their dependence on them. But the fact is that destruction of the rainforests is a global problem. The world has become a small place. What

(opposite page) Youths protest the use of beef produced in demolished rainforest areas.

91

"It's great! You just tell him how much pollution your company is responsible for and he tells you how many trees you have to plant to atone for it"

Ed Fisher © 1989 The New Yorker Magazine. Reprinted by permission.

one nation does affects all other nations. The developed nations are right to speak out, but they must also act to save the rainforests. International cooperation is the only way to ensure a decent future for our planet.

Conserving the rainforest

A number of new international groups are already working on the problem. In 1984, the developing countries that export lumber joined with the developed countries that import lumber and formed the International Tropical Timber Organization (ITTO) to try to find ways to log in the rainforest without destroying it. In 1988, ITTO

Wood from the rainforest is exported for many uses, including the extraction of essential oils, used in making perfumes, cosmetics, shampoos, and foods.

approved a plan to set aside 267,000 acres of rainforest in Brazil as a pilot project. The project is designed to test how effective a managed plan of selective logging and replanting can be. It will be several years before the results are known.

In January 1990, a workshop in Manaus, Brazil, brought together politicians from all the South American rainforest countries and scientists from all over the world. It was the first time everyone concerned with the Amazon rainforest met to discuss the problems. The result was a plan to regulate development in as much as 80 percent of the Amazon rainforest. The plan will be difficult to enforce, but it has the support of the South American governments and offers hope for future conservation programs.

Cultural Survival, a group based in Boston, is trying to prove that profits can be made from the rainforest without destroying it. They are beginning to have success selling products made from nuts, roots, fruits, oils, and essential oils that can be harvested from the rainforest without harming it. Brazil nuts are used to make many of the prod-

Brazilian Indians relax by the river after a day's work in the forest. Many natives depend on the rainforest for their food and livelihood.

ucts, such as a brittle candy called Rainforest Crunch that is also used in cookies and ice cream. Oil from the nuts is the basis for an organic hair conditioner.

In May 1990, seven U.S. senators invited government officials from around the world to an international conference on a number of global environmental problems. Two hundred people from forty-two nations came, and one of the problems they discussed was deforestation. As a result, another international conference was planned to discuss just the protection of forests. Experts feel very optimistic about the fact that so many influential politicians have recognized the need for action. Another action they suggested was to find ways to help the developing nations economically.

Certainly, the developing nations' most critical need is to improve their economies. Without that, the need to destroy rainforest for profit cannot end. One way the world can improve those countries' economies is to help them reduce their foreign debt. In 1984, Dr. Thomas Lovejoy, then vice-president of a conservation group called World Wildlife Fund, came up with an interesting idea called debt-for-nature swaps. Using grants, as well as funds collected from members, conservation groups buy, at a discount, part of a country's debt from the bank that loaned the money. The country, in return for the reduction of its debt, agrees to set aside the same amount of money for a specified conservation project. The first debt-for-nature swap was negotiated between the country of Bolivia and a conservation group called Conservation International (CI) in July 1987. CI bought up $650,000 of Bolivia's $4.5 billion foreign debt, and Bolivia agreed to create a rainforest reserve. Logging companies would be given the right to log in the reserve, but they could take only mahogany trees and then only if they planted trees to replace them. The United

Scenes such as this devastated landscape in burned-out Rondonia, Brazil, have prompted government officials and conservation groups to initiate programs to save the rainforest.

A section of the Amazon rainforest is slashed-and-burned to clear land for cattle ranching and farming.

Will the lush landscape of Brazil cease to exist, or will new trends eradicate rainforest destruction?

Nations hailed this swap as a promising new trend that honored both the need for conservation and the need for development.

Unfortunately, the project has not gone as smoothly as hoped. In the first place, the logging companies have taken out thousands of trees, but native tribes report that they have not yet planted a single replacement. Second, the three native tribes that live in the reserve were not consulted about the swap. They use the mahogany trees to build homes and canoes and resent the fact that the loggers were given rights to all the trees. They are also worried that settlers will follow the logging roads and begin clearing their land for fields.

Various conservation groups have since negotiated similar swaps with other rainforest countries, including Ecuador, Madagascar, Costa Rica, the Philippines, and Zambia in Africa. In November 1989, the debt-for-nature concept received a big boost when the U.S. Congress passed the Global Environmental Protection Assistance Act that authorizes the U.S. government to use money earmarked for foreign assistance to negotiate swaps. Experts are enthusiastic about the potential these swaps have for preserving primary rainforest, but the concept is still too new for the final results to be known.

Stopping slash-and-burn farming

Another problem that must receive immediate attention is the need for alternative food sources and better farming methods for the people in the developing nations. The steady march of slash-and-burn farming across the world's rainforests must be stopped. Four interesting possibilities are being researched by scientists from the Smithsonian Tropical Research Institute (STRI) in Washington, D.C.

One project involves green iguanas, large reptiles that live in the canopy and eat leaves, and pacas, large rodents that feed on nuts and fruits on the forest floor. Both are a good source of protein and, when they can be caught, are eaten by much of the population in Latin America. The STRI is looking for the best way to raise these animals commercially. They are also looking into aquaculture, or raising plants and fish in ponds and lakes. The floating fern that clogs up dams could, for example, be harvested as a fertilizer for gardens to prolong the life of the fields. Other waterweeds could provide food for another good source of protein, fish and turtles, which could be raised commercially.

Forest gardens

Forest gardening is another STRI project. This type of gardening is based on the practice of some native tribes in New Guinea and elsewhere. They plant many small garden plots scattered throughout the rainforest instead of clearing large fields. Planted with a variety of crops, these small

A bulldozer clears brush for a tree plantation in the African rainforest.

plots blend into the ecosystem, so the crops are better protected against disease and insects. The scientists are also experimenting with ways to maintain the fertility of the soil in these gardens. For one thing, they are using leaf litter and other plant matter from the surrounding rainforest as fertilizer. They are also building moats around the gardens to catch rainwater so it will soak back into the soil instead of eroding it and washing all the nutrients away.

Forest gardens could also be used to promote something called garden hunting. Gardens in the rainforest attract animals who find the crops an easy source of food. This makes the animals easier to hunt. The STRI is planting gardens with crops they hope will attract certain animals, particularly deer, pacas, capybaras, and peccaries. All these animals are a good potential food source.

Since logging for both lumber and fuel is the

cause of so much deforestation, experts are now giving more attention to planting timber plantations. Lumber trees are being planted in areas outside the rainforest, in the hope they will not be attacked by diseases and insects. Experts are experimenting to see which trees grow the fastest and which are the easiest to maintain. Logging companies like this idea because it would be much easier and cheaper to cut down trees spaced neatly in rows in a convenient location. Villages are also being encouraged to plant community tree lots that would provide the villagers with fuelwood. A group in Kenya, Africa, has set a good example of action on the local level. The Kenya Energy Non-Governmental Organizations (KENGO) was formed by concerned people from various churches, universities, and clubs in Kenya. Its purpose is to plant trees, and they accomplished more in their first two years than the government did in five. They are also experimenting with different species of trees to see which will grow the best on fuelwood plantations.

Research is the key

New technology could also decrease the use of wood for fuel. More efficient stoves, for instance, would decrease the amount of wood needed for cooking. Instead of charcoal, factories could use compressed pellets of dried-out wood. They burn three to six times longer than charcoal and cause less pollution. Since it is usually the developed nations that develop such new technology, they must share their knowledge with the rainforest countries.

Research of all kinds is one of the main answers to the problem of saving the rainforest. The most essential research involves seeking answers to the way the ecosystem works. Since most of

A rainforest exhibit in the aviary of the San Diego Zoo in California. Such exhibits may help to educate the public about the many dangers facing the rainforest.

the life and mystery of the rainforest lies in the canopy, scientists who want to study it must first find a way to reach it. The canopy is mainly out of sight behind a thick cover and is more than two hundred feet off the ground. And the way up is a hazardous, almost unnavigable maze. Each tree itself is a jungle of moss, ferns, lichens, flowers, vines, insects, snakes, and thorns. To overcome these difficulties, scientists have built walkways from tree to tree high among the leaves. They have sat in suspended seats and hoisted themselves up with special cables, and they have

The canopy of the rainforest lies more than two hundred feet above ground, over a thick tangle of vegetation. Scientists use special cables and suspended seats to hold themselves up so that they can study the rich diversity of life in the canopy.

Scientists know that erosion is just one of the effects of deforestation and are working to salvage such ravaged landscapes.

flown over the canopy in hot-air balloons. They are struggling to learn as much as they can while there is still time. But there are only about fifteen hundred rainforest experts in the world, and it is estimated that it would take the lifetimes of twenty-five hundred scientists just to find and catalog all the plants and animals in the rainforest.

Other scientists are working on a potentially rewarding research project trying to determine the minimum critical size of a rainforest. Since destruction is breaking the primary rainforest up into separate "islands" of varying sizes, scientists want to find out just how large an area of rainforest the ecosystem needs to survive. The minimum critical size is the smallest amount of primary rainforest that could survive intact. In Brazil,

Roads that cut through the trees damage the fragile ecosystem of the rainforest. Unless settlers and natives change their actions, the rainforest will be irreparably damaged.

about fifty miles north of Manaus, Brazilian and American scientists are studying rainforest islands of four sizes: 2.5 acres, 25 acres, 250 acres, and 2,500 acres. They plan to study an island of 25,000 acres in the future.

The research has not been going on long enough for many results to be in, but a few findings are already certain. For example, the 2.5-acre and 25-acre islands have not survived as primary rainforest. The fragile closed system was too badly disturbed. This is because the edges of an area of rainforest get more sun and wind than the interior. They become hotter and drier as far as one hundred yards in from the clearing, which kills many plant and animal species. The sunlight encourages junglelike growth on the floor. The wind knocks over the dried-out, shallow-rooted trees on the edges, letting the sun and wind even farther into the island. New species of sun-loving birds and insects replace the species that normally live there. Plants cannot reproduce because the species that pollinate them are gone. These is-

Scientists are working to save all species of plants and animals from extinction. Establishing national parks and nature reserves to protect the living creatures is just one important step.

lands have become almost all edge, or the changed ecosystem near the clearings. The primary rainforest has been replaced by a secondary one in a matter of months. Even the 250-acre island does not seem big enough to survive. It is now 70 percent edge.

Since the project is scheduled to run until 1999, no one knows yet just what the minimum critical size is. Moreover, it varies for different species. It would probably take more than one million acres to support a jaguar population, for example. That is because jaguars are loners that range over large territories in search of food, and each jaguar must have its own territory. What is clear is that establishing small parks and reserves will not save the rainforest.

The scientists on this project made another discovery that may help preserve the rainforest. They have learned that leaving corridor zones of primary rainforest between islands, thereby linking them together, encourages some species of insects, birds, and small animals to move freely from island to island. This helps maintain both the diversity of species the ecosystem needs and the diversity of genes that keeps each species strong.

Gene banks

Genes from the rainforest are another major interest to scientists. They are fighting to save all the animals and plants from extinction, but they are already losing that battle. Now they are doing the next best thing. They are forming gene banks of endangered species. Gene banks are places where the eggs and sperms of animals and the seeds of plants are preserved for future use, usually by freezing. Then if a domesticated crop gets too weak to fend off insects, the chemical compounds from its stronger, but extinct ancestor will

LIVING SPECIES THE RAINFORESTS SUSTAIN

	PERCENTAGE OF WORLD POPULATION	NUMBER OF DISTINCT SPECIES
FLOWERING PLANTS	0　　　　　50　　　　　100	**112,000** SPECIES
BIRDS		**2,700** SPECIES
PRIMATES		**204** SPECIES
INSECTS	**PERCENTAGE UNKNOWN**	at least **30 Million** SPECIES

Source: Conservation International, Washington, D.C.

be available to save it.

Another research project that experts hope will prove beneficial is the search for the best way to regrow rainforests. Rainforests that have been turned into wastelands are gone forever. The soil is too badly damaged for anything to grow. But some cleared farmland can be salvaged. Scientists are investigating the best methods for planting trees to replace those cut down, but they face a number of problems. For example, they must learn how to duplicate the characteristics of the rainforest ecosystem, or the forest that grows from the planted trees will not be nearly as complex as a primary rainforest. Also, they must find a way to lure animals onto the land to pollinate the plants. One World Wildlife Fund project is now trying to find out whether the complexity of primary rainforest will regenerate more quickly if the trees are planted near an existing rainforest island. They hope that the islands will attract animals that disperse seeds and that those animals will drop seeds from a wide variety of species on the newly planted land.

Unlike cleared land, secondary rainforest can

regenerate itself if it is protected. Even so, experts estimate that it would take at least one hundred years for secondary rainforest to regain anything like the complex mixture of species present in a primary rainforest. The sad thing is that, in the end, it is possible that primary rainforest can never be restored once it is disturbed. Six hundred years ago, much of the rainforest was cleared around Angkor Wat, an ancient city in Cambodia. Although the rainforest that grew up in the clearing has not been disturbed since, it is still different from the rainforest that surrounds it.

The fundamental concern of scientists is that there will not be enough time for all this research to be completed so that the results can be used to save the rainforest. They have called for a moratorium, a temporary halt, to deforestation to give them the time they need, but that will not happen. As an alternative, they are concentrating on educating people about the rainforest, for if enough people become concerned and act, it can make a difference.

Parks and nature reserves

One thing scientists are certain of is that establishing national parks and nature reserves is an important step toward saving the rainforest. There is now a total of about 130,000 square miles of rainforest preserved in parks and reserves, and more are planned. That is not nearly enough to save the rainforest, but is a start. Many of those areas have been selected either because they are particularly endangered by development or because they contain endangered species. Unfortunately, declaring an area a park does not necessarily remove the danger. Many of the parks are "paper parks"; although they were declared reserves on paper, they are not being protected. The governments often do not have the money to pro-

Rock star Sting meets with an Amazonian tribal chief to discuss rainforest issues. Celebrity involvement in initiatives to save the rainforest has encouraged the public to join in protests.

vide the directors, guards, and rangers needed to mark the boundaries and patrol them. Unprotected parks soon fill up with illegal farms, logging operations, mines, and poachers.

One idea that may help prevent illegal activities in parks was initiated by the United Nations Educational, Scientific, and Cultural Organization (UNESCO). It is a new way of designing parks that takes both the needs of people and the needs of the ecosystem into account. These new parks are called either multiuse or biosphere reserves. Multiuse reserves consist of, usually, three zones or rings of land arranged in concentric circles.

Each zone has a different use. The inner zone, or core, is a circle of primary rainforest that is off-limits to everyone. The two outer rings are called buffer zones because they protect the inner core. The middle zone is an extractive reserve where local people may extract, or harvest, wild plants without harming the ecology. No deforestation is allowed. This zone is also open to tourists and scientists conducting research. In the outer zone, local people live, farm, and gather wood. Commercial logging is not permitted inside the reserve. The local people who live in the buffer zones are included in the planning and serve as guardians of the rainforest core.

Strangely enough, one of the ways the developing countries can help preserve their rainforests is to encourage people to visit them. Tourists who visit the parks bring money into the economy. Tourism has become a large source income for all of Rwanda, and the project has accomplished its goals.

Conservation groups

It will take many more national parks and reserves than currently exist to ensure the survival of the rainforest, but, more important, the parks that already exist must be protected. This will happen only if the rainforest nations can be persuaded to commit money for that purpose. There are signs that this will happen. The voices of local and international conservation groups are beginning to be heard throughout the world. Their publicity campaigns are putting pressure on the politicians who must please their public in order to get reelected, and the politicians appear to be responding. In late March 1990, the new Brazilian president, Fernando Collor de Mello, accompanied the army by helicopter into the Roraima territory where the *garimpeiros* are destroying the

An Amazon gold prospector sells his find for a handful of cash. In 1990, Brazilian President Fernando Collor de Mello attempted to halt illegal mining operations by dynamiting miners' airstrips.

rainforest ecosystem with their illegal gold mines. While there, he ordered the troops to dynamite more than one hundred of the miners' airstrips. In addition, Collor has given Brazil's environmental protection agency, called Ibama, a budget of sixty-two million dollars for 1990, more than twice the budget it had for 1989.

Tribal unity

In February 1989, a landmark meeting took place in Brazil. Six hundred natives from a number of tribes that have traditionally been enemies met for five days to discuss the government's proposal to build a huge dam in their region. It was the first time the tribes had ever organized such a meeting, and it was attended by scientists, environmentalists, and reporters from all over the world. In fact, it was the largest environmental meeting ever held in Brazil. It ended with the tribes' determination to stand together in their protest against the dam. Whether or not they will be successful remains to be seen.

Actions like these are encouraging to the experts who believe a strong grassroots, or local, movement for conservation by the people of the rainforest countries could help save the rainforests. It is one of the most effective ways to make sure development and conservation are evenly matched in government policies. Also, for humanitarian reasons, many people believe that native tribes deserve the right to choose how they want to live. This means that if a tribe chooses to retain its own culture, an area of land large enough to sustain that culture should be reserved for them. Laws should be passed to ensure their land is not taken from them or harmed in any way. If a tribe chooses to adopt modern civilization, it should be allowed to do so at its own pace. Most people can adapt to another culture if they do not have it thrust at them too quickly. Unfortunately, this all takes time, and experts are concerned there will not be enough time to save many of these tribes.

Chico Mendes

The plight of the other Amazon rainforest people, the rubber tappers, also received a great deal of publicity in 1989. Unfortunately, it happened because of the death of a *seringueiro* named Chico Mendes. Mendes first became known to the outside world in 1987 when he won an award

Chico Mendes was an advocate of the preservation of the Amazon jungle before he ran into conflict with loggers and ranchers. In 1988, he was murdered by a rancher's son.

Protesters demonstrate against rainforest destruction. Experts are hopeful that public protest will help save the rainforests.

from the United Nations Environment Program. For ten years, as the founder and leader of the *seringueiros* union, he had dedicated himself to trying to get twelve extractive reserves, covering a total of five million acres, established in the rainforest. The rubber tappers and other nut gatherers would receive long-term harvesting rights, and logging and farming would not be permitted. By doing this, he was trying to preserve both the rainforest and his people's way of life. But he ran into conflict with the ranchers who wanted to clear the land for their cattle. On December 22, 1988, he stepped out the back door of his house and was gunned down by a rancher's son. His murder made him an ecological martyr. A television documentary was made about his life, and studios in Hollywood are competing for the right to make his story into a movie. Because of Chico Mendes, Brazil has established four extractive reserves covering a total area of 8,351 square miles since January 1990 and is working on establishing ten more. And also because of him, many more people in the developed nations are fighting to save the rainforest.

It is a challenging fight and a big responsibility, involving many difficult decisions. The U.S. government has many uses for its limited supply of funds. If we want the government to spend money to save the rainforests, are we willing to go without improved roads, new schools, or aid to our elderly to allow them to do it? Or are we willing to pay additional taxes? Are we willing to do without hamburgers to help cut down on deforestation caused by cattle ranching? Would we be willing to sit on chairs made of plastic instead of teak to help stop the destruction from logging? Indeed, some of the choices are more complicated than that. For those who fear that plastic is destroying the atmosphere and also worry paper production is destroying the rainforest, the choice between paper and plastic bags in the grocery story is a real dilemma.

If the world does not take action today, however, there will be no tomorrow in the rainforest. We should acknowledge the developing countries' increasing commitment to rainforest preservation and the advances that are being made. But we should not become so optimistic that we become complacent and quit fighting. Neither should we listen to those who say it is too late to save the rainforest. If we believe that, there is no reason to fight. We should take our clue from the rainforest. It has survived for millions of years by adapting. Now people will have to adapt to save the rainforest.

How You Can Help Save the Rainforest

THE RAINFOREST is located far away from the developed nations, and the problems involved in its destruction are so complex, that it is hard to believe that our individual actions can help save it. But they can. Each action on behalf of the rainforest contributes to its preservation. In fact, the rainforest cannot be saved without action by people in the developed nations.

The list of actions below points out some of the things you can do:

1. Educate yourself about the rainforest.

The more you know about the rainforest, the better you will understand what must be done to save it. Read more books about the rainforest and watch nature documentaries on television. Check to see what videos about the rainforest are available for sale or rent. For example, one lively, six-minute video with rap music called "Vanishing Rain Forests" is available from the World Wildlife Fund. Visit zoos and wild animal parks and attend any rainforest programs and lectures they offer. Better still, become a zoo member. Many zoos are

(opposite page) A forklift picks up a 1,400-pound bale of shredded telephone book sections. The shredded paper will by recycled for other uses.

113

now breeding endangered species so they can be released back into the wild, and your membership fee will contribute to that program. Sometimes museums offer rainforest exhibits. Watch for the excellent traveling exhibit called "Tropical Rainforest: A Disappearing Treasure" that is organized by the Smithsonian Institution in cooperation with the World Wildlife Fund.

2. Educate others about the rainforest.

Share your knowledge with your friends and family. Try to get them involved. Prepare your own exhibit on the rainforest for a school project or science fair. Many rainforest plants make excellent houseplants. Set aside a sunny spot in your house to display your own little rainforest. Start a rainforest club or organization to spread the word.

3. Join organizations that are working on rainforest preservation.

There are now a number of national and worldwide environmental groups that are working to save the rainforest. Your membership fee will contribute to that work, and you will receive regular literature that will keep you up-to-date on what is happening in the rainforest. A partial list of those organizations is included at the end of this section.

4. Become a wise consumer.

The developed nations' demand for lumber, paper, beef, and other products is the cause of much of the deforestation. That means your buying habits affect the rainforest. Ask questions and learn where things come from before you buy them. For example, buy plantation woods such as pine instead of rainforest woods such as teak and mahogany. Recycle paper and cardboard, along with plastic and aluminum cans. Try not to patronize fast food restaurants that buy their beef from ranches located in the rainforests. Do not buy pets (monkeys, parrots, and other exotic birds, for example) that may have been taken from the rainforest illegally. Become more aware of the ban on products from endangered species, such as elephant ivory, leopard skins, and rhinoceros horns. It is now illegal to bring these items into the United States, but they are still for sale in some countries.

On the other hand, try to encourage the harvesting of products that do not harm the rainforest. When you are shopping, try to buy products that contain natural rubber, Brazil nuts or Brazil nut oil, and other essential oils and rainforest plant products.

5. **Write to your local, state, and federal elected officials and urge them to support rainforest preservation.**

Send a letter to the editor of your local newspaper about the need for everyone's participation in this fight. Write to businesses that sell products contributing to deforestation and tell them your concerns. Perhaps they could find alternative sources for their products. Ask everyone you know to write letters, also. Suggest to your science teacher that writing letters to the president of the Untied States about the importance of the rainforests might make a good class project.

Glossary

aborigine: One of the original or earliest known inhabitants of a region or country.

albedo effect: The reflection of the sun's heat off the earth and back into space.

alga (pl. algae): An organism that lives in water and is plantlike but has no true roots, stems, or leaves.

anthropologist: A scientist who specializes in the study of people, their origins, cultures, customs, and beliefs.

aquaculture: growing food, fish, and other crops in water.

bacteria: One-celled, microscopic organisms that are present everywhere in nature and are involved in the process of natural decay, or decomposition.

biological pest control: The use of insect-eating insects to get rid of other insect pests on crops.

bromeliad: One of a wide variety of tropical plants, usually epiphytes, that have long, stiff leaves and showy flowers.

buffer zones: The outer zones of a multiuse reserve used by people and designed to protect the inner core of rainforest.

canopy: The top layer of the rainforest that extends from the top of the understory to the top of the tallest trees.

capybara: A tailless rodent with partly webbed feet that lives on riverbanks; the world's largest rodent.

cerrado: A grassy, treeless plain that surrounds the rainforest in Brazil.

chloroquine: A synthetic chemical based on quinine used to treat malaria.

cloud forest: A rainforest that grows on mountains and is almost always shrouded in clouds and mist.

core: The inner zone of a multiuse reserve that consists of untouchable primary rainforest.

corridor zone: A strip of rainforest that connects two separate areas of rainforest.

debt-for-nature swap: An agreement in which an organization buys part of a country's foreign debt in exchange for which the country establishes a rainforest reserve.

deforestation: Destruction of rainforest, usually by cutting or burning down the trees.

dominant culture: The culture of the government or ruling class in a country.

ecosystem: The interrelationships among all parts of one particular environment, including all natural events and all living things.

epiphyte: A plant that lives on another plant without harming it.

equatorial rainforest: Rainforest near the equator that is hot and rainy all year; also called tropical rainforest.

extractive reserve: A reserve in which only harvesting of products that does not harm the rainforest is allowed.

floor: The bottom layer of the rainforest extending from the ground up to the understory.

forest gardening: Planting small garden plots in the middle of the rainforest.

fungus (pl. fungi): A one-celled or multicellular organism that lives by decomposing and absorbing the organism in which it grows.

garden hunting: Planting crops to attract certain animals that can then be easily hunted for food.

garimpeiros: Independent, often illegal, gold prospectors in the Amazon rainforest.

gene bank: Laboratories where the eggs and sperms of animals and the seeds of plants are preserved by freezing for future use.

geophysicist: A scientist who specializes in the branch of geology that deals with the physics of the earth and its atmosphere.

greenhouse effect: A gradual rise in the earth's temperature over a span of years, caused by heat trapped in gases in the earth's atmosphere.

indigenous: A plant, animal, or person who is native to a particular region or country.

jungle: See secondary rainforest.

latex: A milky liquid in rubber trees that hardens when it is exposed to air.

liana: Woody climbing plants or vines.

lichen: A plantlike, usually green, gray, or yellow organism, composed of both an alga and a fungus, that grows on rocks, tree trunks, and leaves.

mangrove forest: A forest of mangrove trees that grows along the seacoast and is flooded by the tide every day.

metabolism: The sum of all the physical and chemical processes in an organism that makes energy available to that organism.

microorganism: Any organism too small to be seen by the naked eye.

mimicry: A survival technique in which a harmless species looks like a dangerous species.

minimum critical size: The smallest area of primary rainforest in which the ecosystem can survive intact.

multiuse reserve: A reserve that has a core of untouchable primary rainforest surrounded by two or more buffer zones.

niche: The position or function an organism has in a community of plants and animals.

nutrient: A chemical substance that organisms consume for food.

organism: A single living thing, such as a plant, animal, or microorganism.

parasite: An organism that lives on or in another organism of a different species and gets its nutrients from its host, thereby often killing it.

primary forest: Rainforest that has never been disturbed, so the ecosystem remains intact.

quinine: A chemical in the bark of the cinchona tree that cures malaria.

secondary compound: A chemical in a plant that protects it in various ways.

secondary forest: A rainforest whose canopy trees have been cut down, thereby causing junglelike growth on the floor and changing the ecosystem; also called jungle.

selective logging: Cutting down only a few selected trees in an area for lumber instead of cutting down all the trees.

seringueiro: A rubber-tree tapper in the Amazon rainforest.

shifting cultivation: A form of farming in which fields are used for a few years and then left to grow wild for ten years or more until the vegetation can be burned to restore the soil's fertility.

siltation: A buildup of soil in bodies of water that is caused by erosion.

slash-and-burn farming: A destructive form of farming in which individual farmers clear and burn new fields in the rainforest every three years or so.

solar radiation: The heat from the sun.

strangler: A woody vine that starts life as an epiphyte and eventually grows so big that it becomes a parasite and kills its host.

sucker root: A shoot from an underground root that rises above ground and provides additional support for the plant.

tapper: A person who taps the rubber trees for latex to make rubber; also called a *seringueiro* in the Amazon.

terpenoid: A compound in plants that gives oil from the plant a distinct smell.

transmigration: A program of resettlement in Indonesia in which people are moved from crowded islands to rainforest land on less populated islands.

tropical moist forest: Rainforest that lies far enough from the equator to have a dry season but is usually called tropical rainforest.

understory: The middle layer of the rainforest between the floor and the canopy.

Organizations to Contact

The following organizations are concerned with the issues covered in this book. All of them have publications or information available for interested readers.

Conservation International
1015 18th Street NW
Suite 1000
Washington, DC 20036

International Institute for Environment and Development—North America
1717 Massachusetts Avenue NW
Suite 302
Washington, DC 20036

National Zoological Park
Smithsonian Institution
Washington, DC 20008

Rainforest Foundation
Department 0101
Los Angeles, CA 90084

Wildlife Conservation International
New York Zoological Society
Bronx, NY 10460

World Wildlife Fund
1250 24th Street NW
Washington, DC 20037

Zoological Society of San Diego
P.O. Box 551
San Diego, CA 92112

Suggestions for Further Reading

Mary Batten, "The Cradle of Life," *Science Digest,* July 1981.

Catherine Caufield, *In the Rainforest.* New York: Knopf, 1985.

Julie Sloan Denslow and Christine Padoch, eds., *People of the Tropical Rain Forest.* Berkeley: University of California Press, 1988.

Peter Farb, *The Forest.* New York: Time, 1961.

Andrew W. Mitchell, *The Enchanted Canopy.* New York: Macmillan, 1986.

Norman Myers, *The Primary Source: Tropical Forests and Our Future.* New York: W.W. Norton, 1984.

James D. Nations, *Tropical Rainforests: Endangered Environment.* New York: Franklin Watts, 1988.

Ghillian T. Prance, ed., *Tropical Rain Forests and the World Atmosphere.* Boulder, CO: Westview Press, 1986.

P.W. Richards, *The Tropical Rain Forest.* Cambridge, England: Cambridge University Press, 1981.

Michael H. Robinson, "Is Tropical Biology Real?" *Tropical Ecology,* vol. 19, 1978.

Michael H. Robinson, "Alternatives to Destruction: Investigations into the Use of Tropical Forest Resources with Comments on Repairing the Effects of Destruction," *The Environmental Professional,* vol. 7, 1985.

Works Consulted

Lee Durrell, *State of the Ark: An Atlas of Conservation in Action*. New York: Doubleday, 1986.

Adrian Forsyth and Ken Miyata, *Tropical Nature: Life and Death in the Rain Forests of Central and South America*. New York: Scribner's, 1984.

Judith Gradwoh and Russell Greenberg, *Saving the Tropical Forests*. London: Earthscan Publications, 1985.

Terry J. Jennings, *Exploring Our World: Tropical Forests*. Freeport, NY: Marshall Cavendish, 1987.

Norman Myers, *The Sinking Ark: A New Look at the Problem of Disappearing Species*. New York: Pergamon Press, 1979.

V. Perera and R. D. Bruce, *The Last Lords of Palenque: The Lacandon Mayas of the Mexican Rain Forest*. Boston: Little, Brown, 1982.

Colin Turnbull, *The Forest People: A Study of the Pygmies of the Congo*. New York: Simon & Schuster, 1962.

Index

About the Author

Lois Warburton earned her Masters degree in education at Clark University in Worcester, Massachusetts. Her previous published works include nonfiction articles, newspaper and magazine columns, and short stories. She is a past president of The Wordwright, a firm providing writing services to authors, businesses, and individuals. Ms. Warburton is now retired.

Picture Credits